SPSS
QuickStarts

Neil J. Salkind
University of Kansas

Samuel B. Green
Arizona State University

Prentice Hall

Boston   Columbus   Indianapolis   New York San Francisco   Upper Saddle River
Amsterdam Cape Town Dubai London Madrid Milan Munich Paris Montreal Toronto
Delhi   Mexico City   São Paulo   Sydney   Hong Kong   Seoul   Singapore   Taipei   Tokyo

Executive Editor:	Jeff Marshall
Editorial Assistant:	Amy Trudell
Marketing Manager:	Nicole Kunzmann
Marketing Assistant:	Amanda Olweck
Senior Production Project Manager:	Patrick Cash-Peterson
Manufacturing Buyer:	Debbie Rossi
Cover Administrator:	Kristina Mose-Libon
Editorial Production and Composition Service:	Saraswathi Muralidhar, GGS Higher Education Resources, A Division of PreMedia Global Inc.

Library of Congress Cataloging-in-Publication Data

Salkind, Neil J.
  SPSS QuickStarts / Neil J. Salkind, Samuel Green.—1st ed.
    p. cm.
  Includes index.
  ISBN-13: 978-0-205-73577-8
  ISBN-10: 0-205-73577-0
  1. SPSS (Computer file) 2. Social sciences—Statistical methods—Computer programs. I. Green, Samuel B. II. Title.
  HA32.S12195 2011
  005.5'5—dc22

                                                                            2010013071

10 9 8 7 6 5 4 3   13 12

Prentice Hall
is an imprint of

PEARSON
www.pearsonhighered.com

ISBN 10: 0-205-73577-0
ISBN 13: 978-0-205-73577-8

Contents

How to Use SPSS QuickStarts

What Is SPSS

SPSS is a set of data manipulation and statistical analysis programs that are used by researchers and analysts to understand the meaning of their data. While SPSS was once an acronym for Statistical Package for the Social Sciences, the name was changed in early 2009 to Predictive Analytics Software, abbreviated as PASW. SPSS/PASW was then acquired by IBM in October 2009 and the name was returned to SPSS. Throughout this book, we will use SPSS to represent this package of programs. Please note that SPSS version 18.0 (released under the name PASW) was used to prepare the materials in this book.

What Is *SPSS QuickStarts*?

SPSS QuickStarts is a guide to the skills that behavioral and social science researchers, educational and business analysts, and others use to conduct statistical analyses. It focuses on the SPSS procedures and techniques that these individuals are likely to apply to analyze their data.

SPSS QuickStarts provides you with 37 succinctly written QuickStarts or short chapters that clearly describe and illustrate techniques for analyzing your data. These techniques range in complexity. They include straightforward entry, editing, and manipulation of SPSS data files; simple statistical methods, such as the assessment of differences in means from two independent samples; and more complex statistical analyses, for example, factor analysis to aid in assessing the underlying dimensions for a set of measures.

As indicated by its title, *SPSS QuickStarts*, by design, is intended to offer a series of chapters that prepare you as quickly as possible to analyze your data using a variety of statistical methods. We have designated the 37 chapters as QuickStarts in that they are brief and provide what you need to know to get you up and running in conducting your analyses. The QuickStarts present step-by-step instructions for conducting the various techniques and, where appropriate, identifying the parts of the SPSS output that are key for the interpretation of results.

This book is not intended as a substitute for a complete and thorough treatment of the various SPSS techniques. *SPSS QuickStarts* does not cover the mathematical assumptions underlying the various statistical methods, the multitude of strategies that one may take to arrive at data-driven answers to questions, or the thought process underlying the choices among these strategies. This information is available in statistical textbooks and more detailed books on using SPSS, such as Green and Salkind's *Using SPSS for Windows and Macintosh*, also published by Prentice-Hall.

What's in *SPSS QuickStarts*?

While you can begin at any point in *SPSS QuickStarts* and learn about using different techniques, the book is organized in nine major sections, including the following.

- SPSS Basics
- Creating an SPSS Data File
- Working with an SPSS Data File
- Creating and Editing SPSS Graphs and Tables

- Descriptive Statistics
- Evaluating Means
- Correlation and Regression
- Discriminant, Factor, and Reliability Analyses
- Nonparametric Statistics

How to Use *SPSS QuickStarts*?

You can use *SPSS QuickStarts* in several ways:

- You can work through the book in a linear fashion, reading each QuickStart one at a time and working through the examples.
- You can locate the specific skills or statistical techniques that you would like to learn about and go to them directly. While some of the later chapters in *SPSS QuickStarts* build on earlier material in the book, for the most part, you can begin anywhere and learn what it is you need to know to conduct a particular statistical procedure.

In using QuickStarts, we recommend you follow these suggestions:

1. Browse through *SPSS QuickStarts* so you can become familiar with how the book is organized and what techniques and skills are covered.
2. If you are learning about a statistical technique for the first time, you should find a book or a course that examines the conceptual underpinnings of the technique and the knowledge necessary to properly apply it.
3. Follow the text in our book very carefully. We use a simple step-by-step approach for going from point A to point B. If something you enter or a procedure does not work, then try it again. If you are taking a course, ask a classmate for assistance.
4. While this book is based on SPSS version 18, it can also be used for earlier versions of SPSS. The screens may look a bit different, but for the most part, the procedural commands and output are very similar. The same is true for the Windows and Macintosh versions. Most procedures are extremely similar if not identical.

The Data Sets

Many of the QuickStarts in this book use data sets that you can download from http://www.prehall.com/ greensaklindqs. These data sets are used in the chapters in our book to illustrate how SPSS procedures are applied and what parts of the results are most pertinent for interpretation.

What You Need to Use SPSS

The software and hardware requirements to use SPSS are as follows.

For Windows

- Microsoft Windows XP (32-bit version), Windows Vista (32-bit and 64-bit versions), or Windows 7 (32-bit and 64-bit versions).
- Intel or AMD processor running at 1 gigahertz (GHz) or higher.
- 1 gigabyte (GB) of RAM or more.
- 675 megabytes (MB) of available hard-disk space. If you install more than one help language, each additional language requires 50–60 MB of disk space.
- DVD drive.

- Super VGA (800x600) or a higher-resolution monitor.
- For connecting with an SPSS Statistics Server, a network adapter running the TCP/IP network protocol.

For Macintosh

- Mac OS® X 10.5 or higher (32- or 64-bit) (Leopard and Snow Leopard).
- Intel processor.
- 1 gigabyte (GB) of RAM or more.
- 925 megabytes (MB) of available hard-disk space. If you install more than one help language, each additional language requires 150–170 MB of disk space.
- DVD drive.
- Super VGA (800x600) or a higher-resolution monitor.
- For connecting with an SPSS Statistics Server, a network adapter running the TCP/IP network protocol.
- Java Standard Edition 5.0 (J2SE 5.0) or 6.0 (J2SE 6.0)

We owe many people a great deal of debt for helping us to make this book as close as we could to what we think it should be. At IBM SPSS, Aaron Rangel and Sarah Tomahawk were very helpful throughout the entire process. At Prentice Hall, Jeff Marshall, executive editor for psychology, helped us go from an idea to a manuscript with the always helpful LeeAnn Doherty.

A Note to Instructors

We realize that one role this book might play is as a supplement to the primary text you may be using. It's for this reason that we have created a table of introductory statistics books and what chapters in *SPSS QuickStarts* might best fit the book you use. You can find this table at http://www.prehall.com/greensaklindqs. We could not possibly include all the introductory statistics books available, but tried to include those that are most popular.

We take responsibility for any, and all, errors. If you find one, please send us an email so we can continue to improve the book for future users.

Finally, this book is dedicated to our children and grandchildren who will make the world a better place for all of us. We have enjoyed writing this book and hope that you find it easy to use and helpful. Please write to us with suggestions and ideas for improvement and any other information you might think will prove useful.

Neil J. Salkind
njs@ku.edu

Sam B. Green
samgreen@asu.edu

PART I   SPSS Basics

QuickStart 1 | Starting SPSS

The process of starting SPSS is identical to other computer programs.

Opening SPSS

You can open SPSS using one of the following techniques.

- Click on the *Start Menu* at the bottom of the desktop. Click *Programs*, and click the SPSS entry among the list of programs.

- Double click on the shortcut icon representing the SPSS program that is on the desktop.

- Double click on an icon representing an existing SPSS data file.

- Find the folder containing the executable file for the SPSS program (e.g., statistics.exe). Double click on the file name.

Initial Choices in SPSS

Once you have opened SPSS, you may see a start up window as shown in Figure 1.1. (It is possible that a previous user has instructed SPSS to not show this dialog box.) Here you can select among a number of options, including running the SPSS tutorial, typing in new data, opening an existing data file, or opening another type of file as specified in the dialog box. When using this book, we recommend clicking *Cancel*. You are now ready to continue.

More ...

Opening SPSS reveals the *Data Editor*, as shown in Figure 1.2. If you look at the bottom-left side of the *Data Editor*, you will see a *Data View* tab and a *Variable View* tab.

- The *Data View* shows the entered data. In this tab, you can enter your data. See QuickStart 6 for more details.

- The *Variable View* shows you the properties of variables. In this tab, you can configure how the data appear in the *Data View* (e.g., alignment of the data in the cells), how to treat the data (e.g., defining missing values in the data), and other properties. See QuickStart 5 for more details.

More windows appear as you work with SPSS. For example, the *Output Window* will contain the results from the statistical analyses that you conduct.

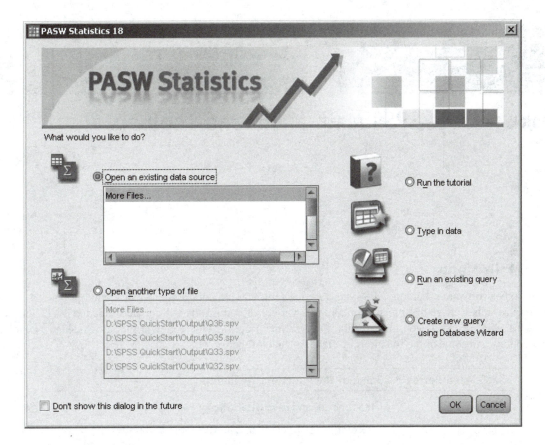

Figure 1.1 SPSS start up dialog box.

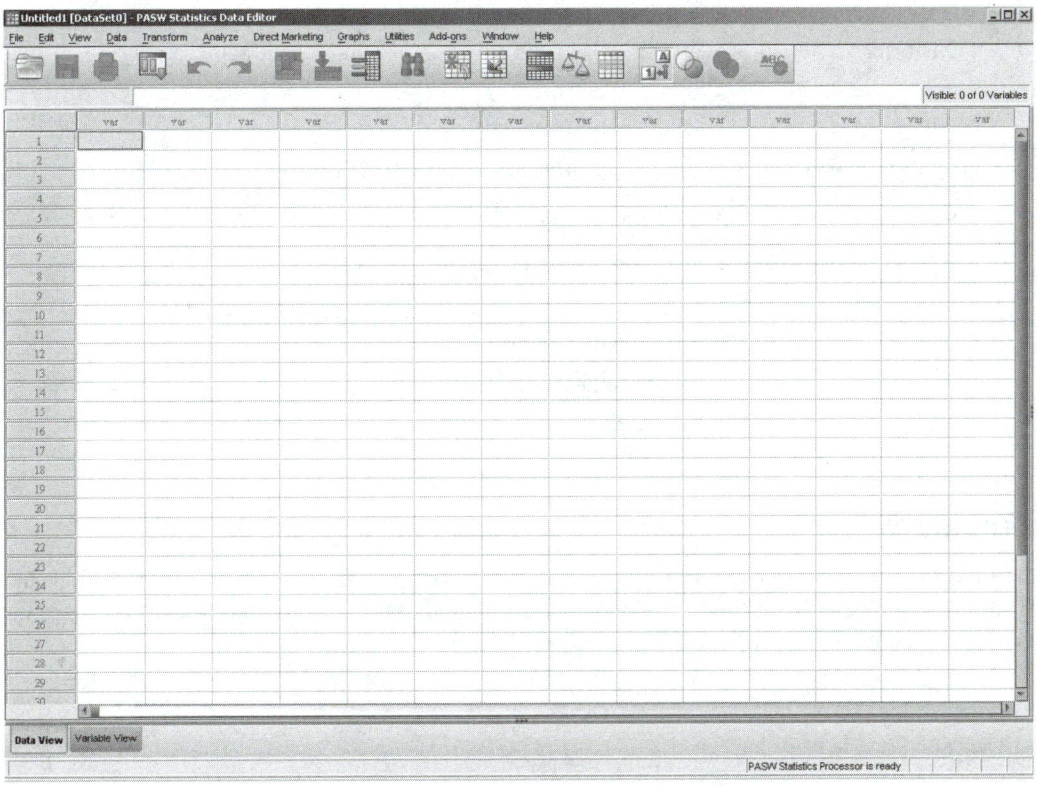

Figure 1.2 *Data Editor* with *Data View* and *Variable View* tabs.

SPSS Main Menu

As with other software programs, SPSS has a *Main Menu* that includes a number of menu options. Clicking on an option reveals a specialized menu containing a variety of commands with related functions. You can see in Figure 2.1 what occurs if you click on the *Analyze* menu option. The following table lists each of the *Main Menu* options and some of the functions available in each of them.

SPSS Menu Option	Some of the Functions Available
File	Create, open, and save SPSS files
Edit	Insert variables or cases in data file; copy and paste data
View	Determine the display of information in the *Data Editor*
Data	Sort cases or variables; select cases; merge, split, or restructure files
Transform	Create variables from existing ones; rank data; replace missing values
Analyze	Conduct analyses of data
Direct Marketing	Specific applications such as direct marketing
Graphs	Create SPSS graphs
Utilities	Access more advanced features in SPSS
Add-ons	Describes SPSS add-ons that are not part of the standard SPSS package, such as *Neural Networks*
Window	Controls display of SPSS Windows
Help	Use SPSS *Help*

SPSS Toolbars

SPSS has a variety of toolbars that can be used to speed up your work. Rather than trying to find the option from the *Main Menu*, you can click on a toolbar icon. Each toolbar is constructed such that when you move the mouse over an icon, its function is revealed, as you see in Figure 2.2.

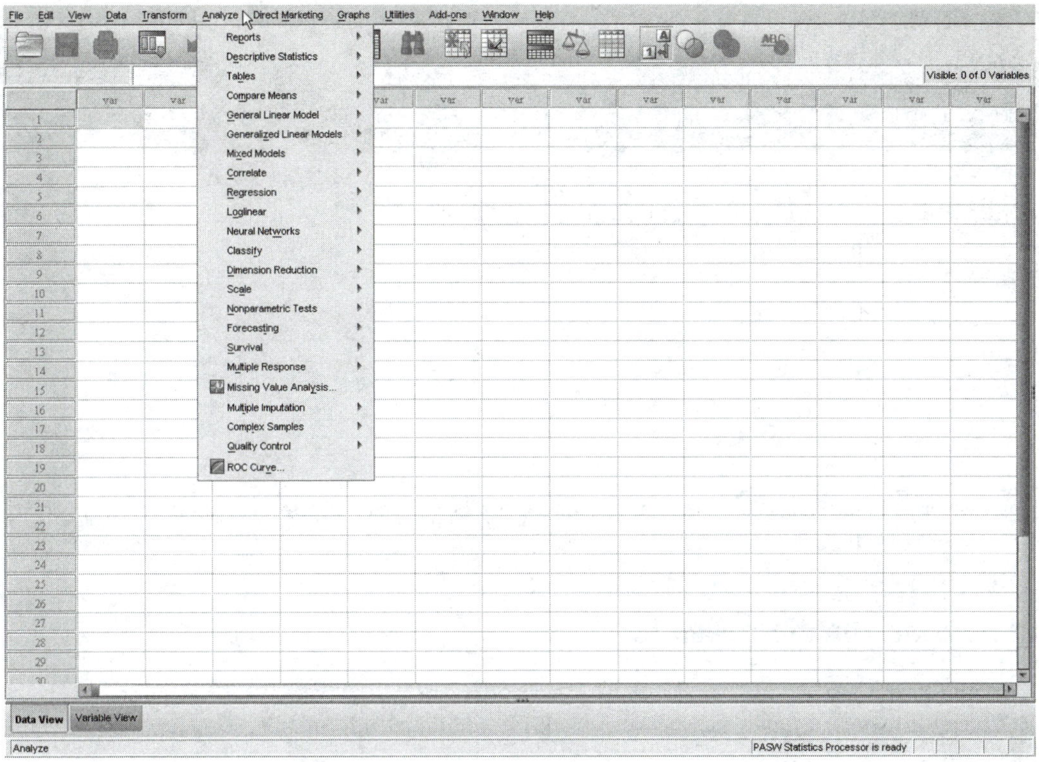

![SPSS Data Editor window showing the Analyze menu open with options including Reports, Descriptive Statistics, Tables, Compare Means, General Linear Model, Generalized Linear Models, Mixed Models, Correlate, Regression, Loglinear, Neural Networks, Classify, Dimension Reduction, Scale, Nonparametric Tests, Forecasting, Survival, Multiple Response, Missing Value Analysis, Multiple Imputation, Complex Samples, Quality Control, ROC Curve.]

Figure 2.1   Options under *Analyze* from the *Main Menu*.

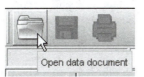

Figure 2.2   Tool tip for an icon on the *Data Editor toolbar*.

QuickStart 3 | Using SPSS Help

SPSS has extensive help menus to assist you in using it effectively and efficiently. There are a several ways to get help, each covered below.

Using *Help* on the *Main Menu*

The *Help* option, the last choice on the *Main Menu*, offers help in a variety of categories, with the most important being a listing of topics that you can click for additional information. To access *Help*, conduct the following steps:

1. Click *Help → Topics*, and you will see a list of topics in the *Contents* tab, as shown in Figure 3.1. You are likely to be interested in topics under the *Core System* and the *Statistics Base* option.

2. Click on a + sign to the left of any topic to expand the topic and see subtopics. As shown in Figure 3.1, if you click on the + sign next to *Data Files*, you see subtopics, such as *Opening Data Files*.

3. Click on a topic or a subtopic, and you will see information about it in the adjoining window.

The *Online Help* window also contains three other tabs that you can use to find more help or to use help in a different way. Here is a summary of each tab and what it does.

Help Tab	What It does
Contents	Provides a listing of Help topics by category
Index	Lists topics in alphabetical order
Search	Allows searches for specific topics
Favorites	Allows the definition of particular help topics for your later use

Using the F1 Function Key

When you are in a dialog box to conduct a particular type of statistical analysis, you may press the F1 key to access help about performing this analysis. In other words, SPSS *Help* is context responsive. In Figure 3.2, you can see the result of pressing the F1 key when you have selected *Analyze → Compare Means → Independent Samples T test*. You can access the same information through the *Help* option on the *Main Menu*, but using F1 is much faster.

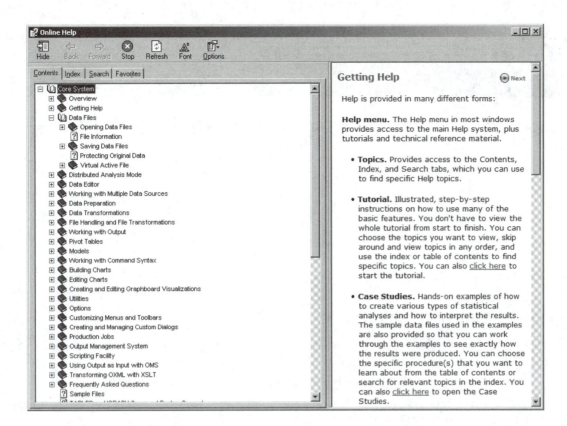

Figure 3.1   Topics in the *Contents* tab in *Help*.

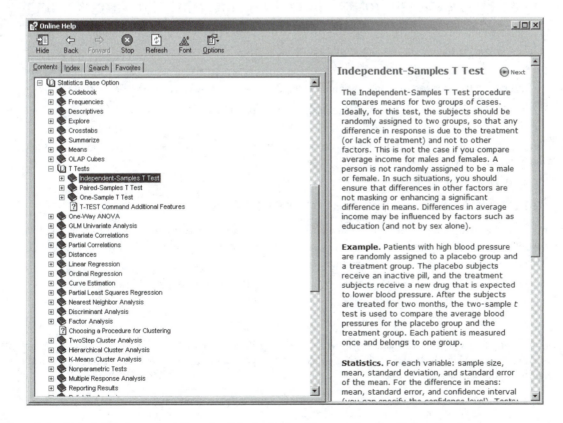

Figure 3.2   Help for Independent-Samples T test obtained by pressing the F1 function key.

QuickStart 4 | Opening and Saving an SPSS Data File

One of the first SPSS skills to learn is opening and saving a new or previously created SPSS data file.

Opening a New SPSS Data File

When you open SPSS (see QuickStart 1), a new data file will open. If you are working within SPSS and you wish to create a new data file, conduct the following steps:

1. Click *File → New → Data*. A new data file will open, as shown in Figure 4.1.

2. You may now enter your data into the cells in the *Data Editor*. Rows represent cases, and columns represent variables. See QuickStart 6 for more information about entering data.

Saving an SPSS Data File for the First Time and While You Are Working

1. After you have entered data, click *File → Save* (or use the Ctrl + S key combination). You will see the *Save Data As* dialog box, as shown in Figure 4.2.

2. Enter a file name for your data file. In addition, specify where you want to save your data file by indicating the location on your computer in the drop down menu near the top of the dialog box.

3. Click *Save*. The file will be saved with a *.sav* extension, which allows you to distinguish it from other files.

Each time you want to save the data file as you are working, you can use the CTRL + S key combination or click the *Save* icon on the toolbar.

Saving an SPSS Data File with a Different Name

You may want to save a data file under another name. For example, if you have made changes to a file, you might want to save the changed file under a new name as well as maintain the original file under its old name. To save a data file with a new name, follow these steps:

1. Click *File → Save As*. You will see the *Save Data As* dialog box, as shown in Figure 4.2.

2. Enter a new name for the file.

3. Click *Save*.

It is critical to save your data as you work. When entering data, save the data file approximately every 5 to 10 minutes. Also, when you finish your SPSS session, store your data in another location such as a flash drive or email it to yourself as an attachment.

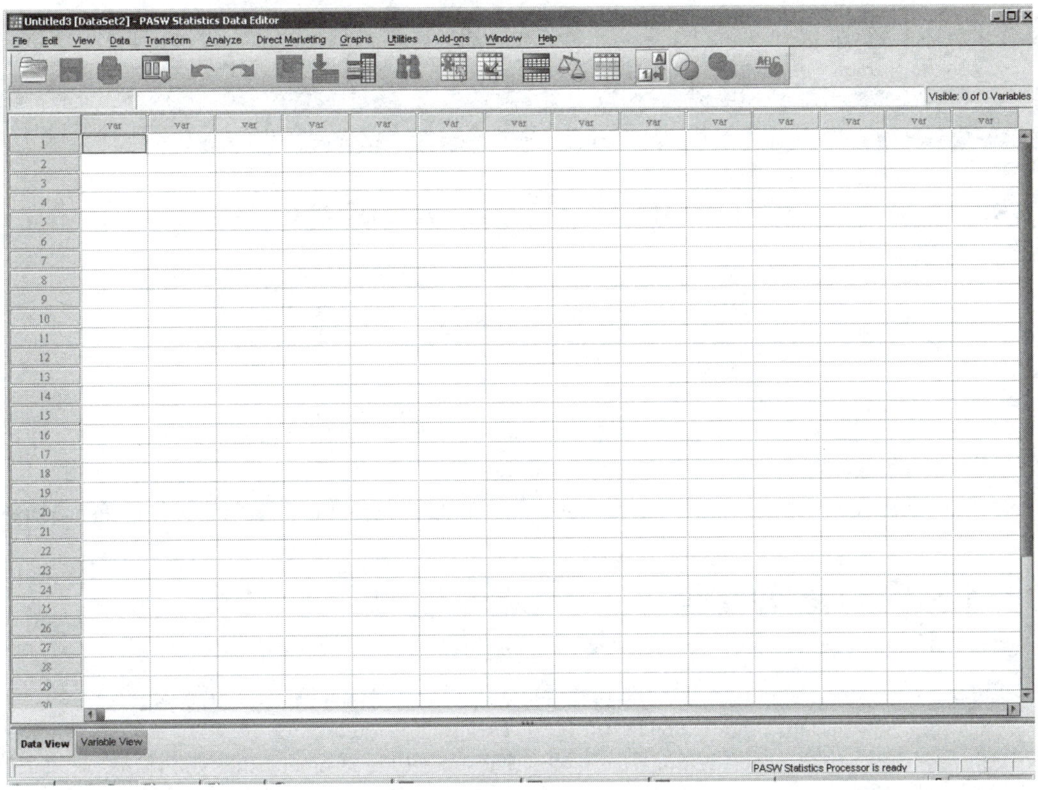

Figure 4.1 New data file available in the *Data Editor*.

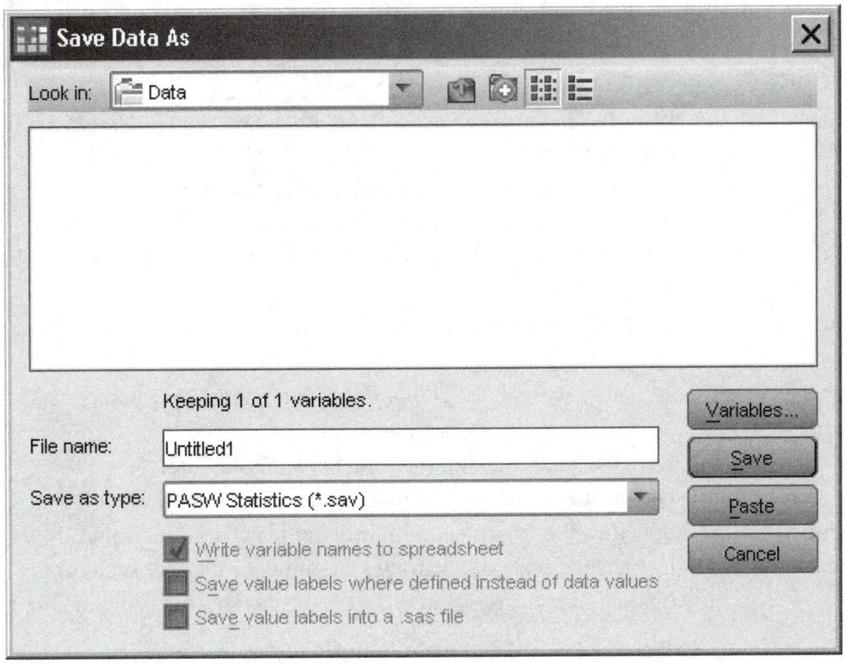

Figure 4.2 *Save Data As* dialog box.

QuickStart 5 | Defining Variable Properties

Before entering data, you should define your variables, including naming them and specifying their properties.

Defining Variable Properties

1. Click *File → New → Data*. You will see the *Data Editor*.

2. Enter a value (e.g., 12) in a cell in the first column and press Enter. SPSS will recognize that you are creating a new variable and name it *VAR00001*, as shown in Figure 5.1. If you enter data in other columns, SPSS will name additional variables. We strongly recommend that you name and define the properties of your variables before you enter your data.

3. Click the *Variable View* tab at the bottom of the *Data Editor*. This tab is shown in Figure 5.2. The properties are described in the table.

Variable Property	What It Does
Name	Specifies the variable name. It should begin with a letter and contain no spaces.
Type	Defines the type of variable, such as text, numeric, or string. A good choice for most applications is numeric.
Width	Defines the number of characters that are shown for a variable in the Data Editor.
Decimals	Defines the number of decimals that are shown for a variable in the Data Editor.
Label	Defines a variable label that is no longer than 256 characters.
Values	Defines labels for the various values of a variable.
Missing	Defines values that are interpreted as missing data.
Columns	Defines the width of a column for a variable in the Data Editor.
Align	Specifies the alignment of values in the cells of the Data Editor.
Measure	Defines the scale of a variable: nominal, ordinal, or scale. It is ignored in many applications.
Role	The role the variable plays in the data set.

4. To define any of the properties shown in the above table, click on the cell and make your selection. For example, in Figure 5.3 you see how variable width was specified to be five characters by clicking on the down arrow. The default is eight.

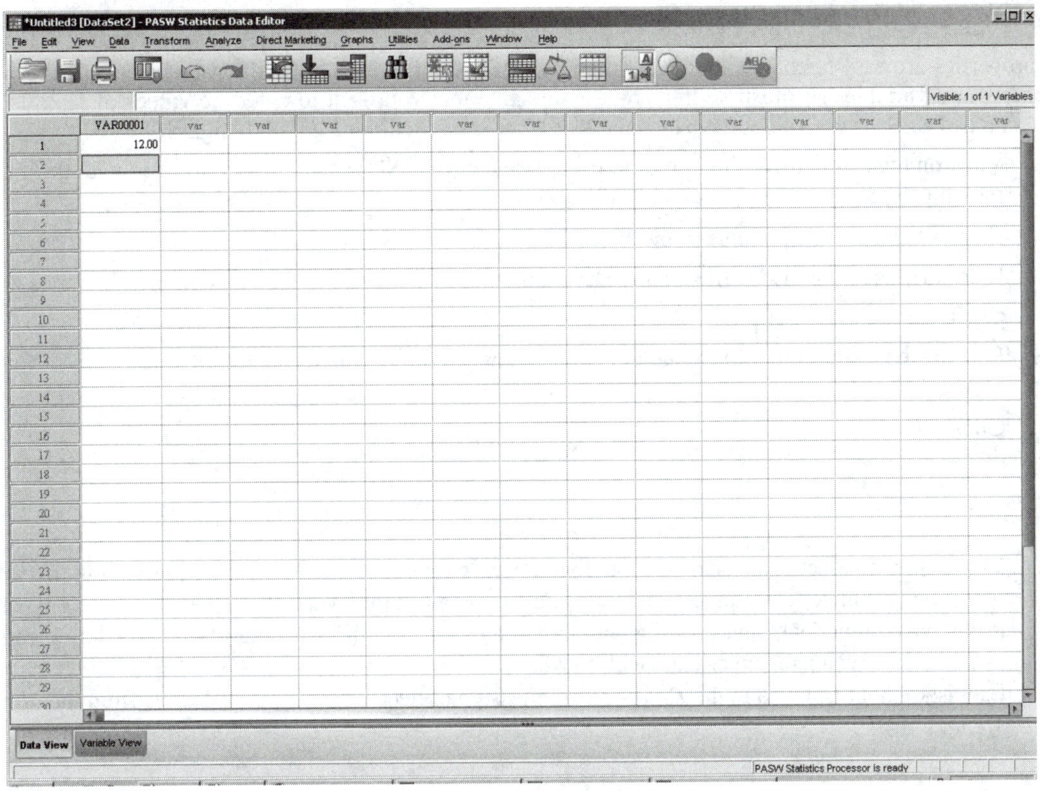

Figure 5.1 Automatic naming of a new variable.

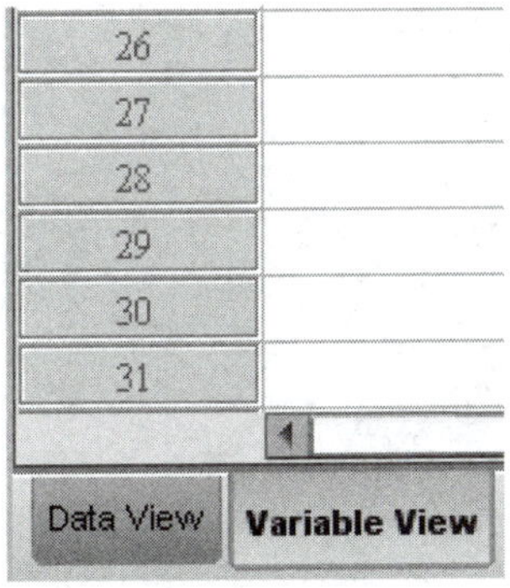

Figure 5.2 *Variable* View tab.

Defining the Property *Values*

Most properties are easy to change, but some may require greater attention. Below, we show steps for defining the values for a variable. To illustrate this process, imagine that you want to enter the values of 1, 2, or 3 for a variable named SES. These values have the labels of Low SES, Medium SES, and High SES.

1. Click on the cell in the *Values* column for a variable (e.g., SES) and click on the box with three dots (an ellipsis) to open the *Value Labels* dialog box.

2. Enter a value for the variable in the *Value* box (e.g., 1).

3. Enter the label (e.g., Low SES) in the *Label* box that corresponds to the value in the *Value* box.

4. Click *Add*.

5. Repeat steps 2 through 4 for remaining values (e.g., 2 and 3). The labels for all values are shown in Figure 5.4.

6. Click *OK*.

More ...

- You cannot conduct some analyses if the variables in those analyses are defined as having particular types. For example, you cannot conduct a one-sample *t* test on a variable defined as a string type, even if you have numerical values for that variable in the *Data Editor*. We suggest that you define variables as numeric as you gain experience with SPSS.

- Labels are not displayed in the *Data Editor* unless you select *View* → *Value Labels* from the *Main Menu*.

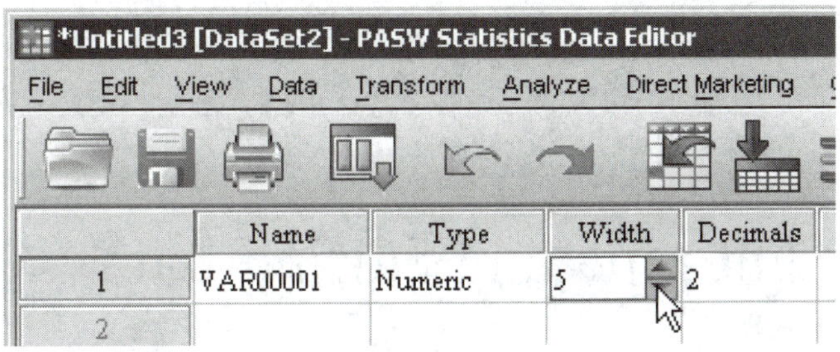

Figure 5.3 Changing the width of a variable.

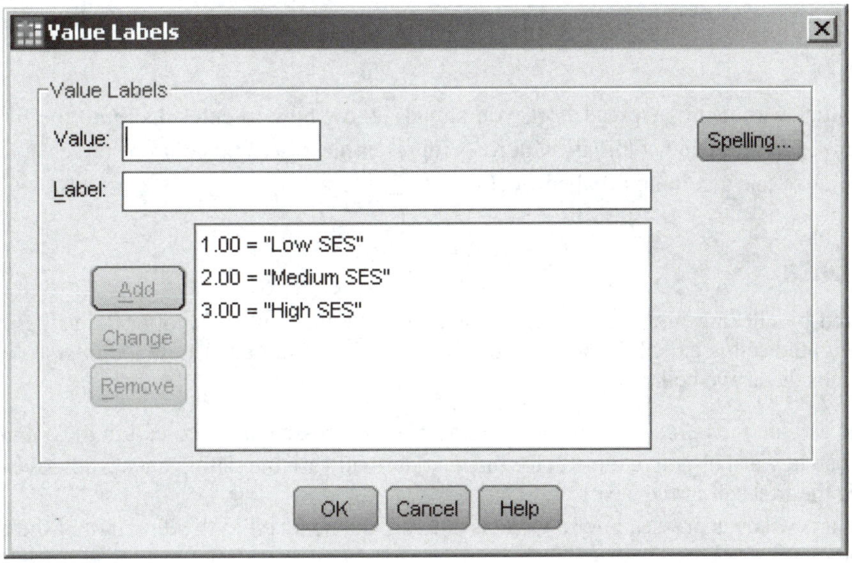

Figure 5.4 *Value Labels* dialog box.

QuickStart 6 | Entering and Editing Data

If you are familiar with using a spreadsheet, you already know how to enter data into the SPSS *Data Editor*. Data are organized by rows and columns, with rows representing cases and columns representing variables. The intersection of a row and a column is called a cell.

Entering Data

Data are entered by clicking in the cell where a value is to be inserted and typing the value in the highlighted cell. The highlighted cell is called the active cell. You can see in Figure 6.1 how the intersection of Row 3 and Column 1 defines the active cell.

- When a value is entered in a cell and the Enter key is pressed, the next cell in the column is active.
- The Tab key makes active the cell for the next defined variable within a row; otherwise, it makes active the first cell in the next row.
- If the arrow key is pressed after a value is entered, the next cell in the direction of the arrow key becomes the active cell.

Editing Data

Editing data is done by locating the particular cell you want to change and then making the change. This can be done in a variety of ways.

- Click on the cell containing the value you want to edit. The cell should be highlighted. Enter the new value and press the Enter key. The new value will replace the old one.
- Double click on the cell containing the value you want to edit. Click to the right of the digit you want to change. Press the Backspace key to delete the current value. Enter the new value.
- Click on the cell containing the value you want to edit. Make changes in the entry bar located near the top of the SPSS data window, as shown in Figure 6.2. Press the Enter key.

More ...

- You may not have complete data for all cases. If you leave a cell blank, it will be replaced with a period. A period represents missing data in SPSS.

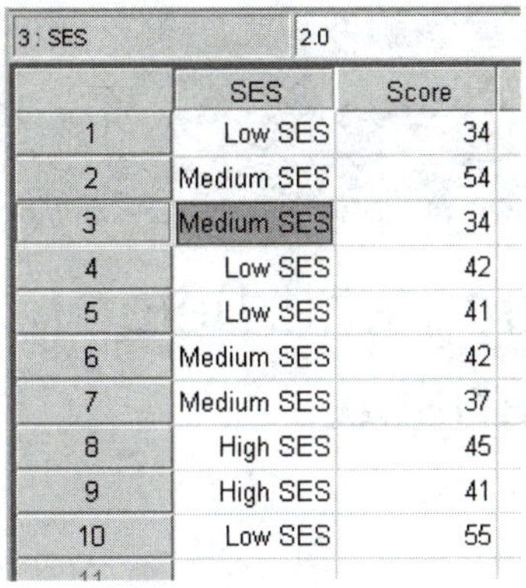

Figure 6.1 Entering data in an active cell.

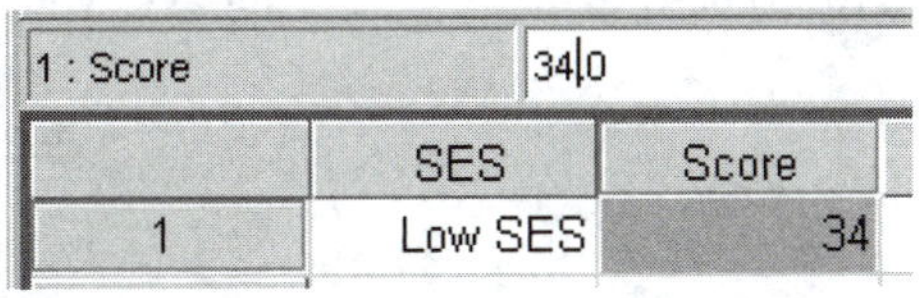

Figure 6.2 Editing data in the data entry bar.

You can easily add new cases (i.e., rows) or variables (i.e., columns) to your data set as well as delete existing cases or variables from it.

The Data

Our example data are in the file named Q7.sav.

Variable	Description
SIS	Social Introversion Scale
PSI	Personal Shyness Index
HSGPA	High School Grade Point Average

The example data includes scores on three measures for 27 high school seniors. With the example data, we illustrate how to insert a case, insert a variable, delete a case, and delete a variable.

Inserting a Case

1. Click on a cell in a selected row (e.g., first cell of case 19). The new case will be inserted immediately following the selected row.
2. Click *Edit → Insert Cases*. A new row is created, as you see in Figure 7.1. You can also insert a new case by clicking on the *Insert Cases* icon on the toolbar.
3. Type in the data for the new case.

Inserting a Variable

1. Click on a cell in a selected column (e.g., first cell of the PSI column). The new variable will be inserted immediately to the left of the selected column.
2. Click *Edit → Insert Variables.* A new column is created, as you see in Figure 7.2. Alternatively, you can insert a new variable by clicking on the *Insert Variable* icon on the toolbar. The name assigned by SPSS to the new variable is VAR00001. You should go to *Variable View* and give it a more meaningful name.
3. Type in the data for the new variable.

14	55	60	2.86
15	44	44	2.49
16	59	49	3.13
17	73	65	2.12
18	31	28	2.01
19	.	.	.
20	56	44	3.09
21	38	43	2.94
22	42	51	2.97
23	49	51	2.03
24	51	50	3.38

Figure 7.1   Inserting a new case.

1 : VAR00001

	SIS	VAR00001	PSI	HSGPA
1	38		38	2.78
2	57	.	44	3.91
3	59	.	66	3.09
4	35	.	49	3.85

Figure 7.2   Inserting a new variable.

Deleting a Case

1. Click on the row (far left, where the rows are numbered) you want to delete. The row should now be highlighted. For example, click on case 10 to highlight it before you delete it, as shown in Figure 7.3.
2. Click *Edit → Clear* to delete the case. Alternatively you could press the Delete key on your keyboard after the row is highlighted.

Deleting a Variable

1. Click on the variable name at the top of the column you want to delete. The column should now be highlighted. For example, click on the PSI column to highlight it before you delete it, as shown in Figure 7.4.
2. Click *Edit → Clear* to delete the variable. Alternatively, the Delete key could be used to delete the variable.

More ...

- If you inadvertently delete a case or a variable, you can restore it by using the *Undo* button on the toolbar or type the Ctrl + Z key combination.
- If you want to delete multiple rows or columns, drag across the multiple rows or columns to select them prior to clicking *Edit → Clear*.

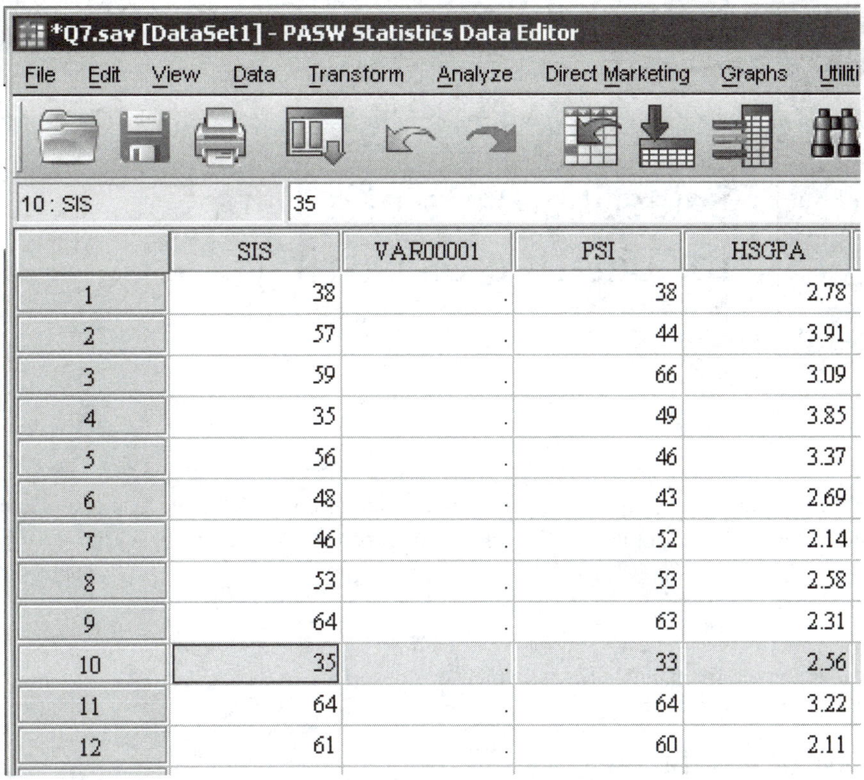

Figure 7.3 Selecting a case to delete it.

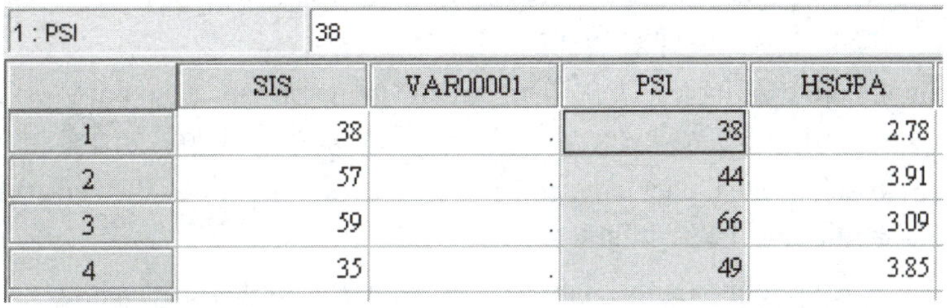

Figure 7.4 Selecting a variable to delete.

Selecting Parts of a Data Set for Deleting or Pasting

Within the SPSS data editor, you can select a part of a data set and then delete it. You can also cut or copy the selected part and then paste it to another location in the same data set or in another data set.

The Data

Our example data are in the file named Q7.sav, which was described in QuickStart 7.

Deleting Part of a Data Set

1. Select cases, variables, or cells to delete.

   - If you want to delete cases, click on a row (far left, where the rows are numbered) and drag your cursor over the rows that you want deleted. These rows should now be highlighted. We selected cases 23, 24, and 25, as shown in Figure 8.1.

   - If you want to delete variables, click on a variable name on top of a column and drag your cursor over the columns that you want deleted. Those columns should now be highlighted.

   - If you want to delete cells, click on a cell and drag your cursor over the cells that you want deleted. Those cells should now be highlighted.

2. Click *Edit → Clear*. For our example, cases 23 through 25 should be deleted.

Cutting or Copying and Then Pasting a Part of a Data Set

1. Select cases, rows, or cells using the same procedures described in step 1 above. We selected variables SIS and PSI, as shown in Figure 8.2.

2. Click *Edit → Cut* or *Edit → Copy*. For our example, SIS and PSI were selected.

3. Click on the rows, columns, or cells where you want the data to appear. It can be in the current data file or in another data file. We selected the column after HSGPA.

4. Click *Edit → Paste*. The selected data will appear in the new location.

More ...

- Always save a data set before you make changes to it in case you encounter problems.

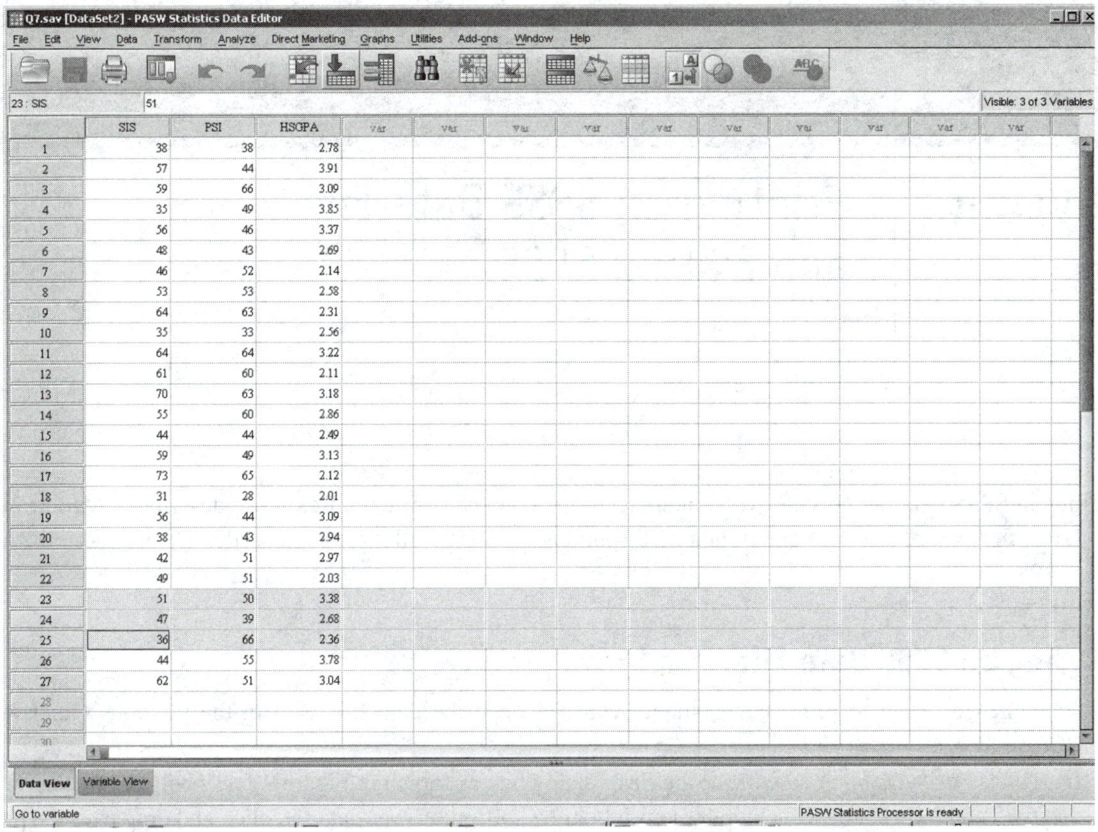

Figure 8.1 Selected cases for deleting.

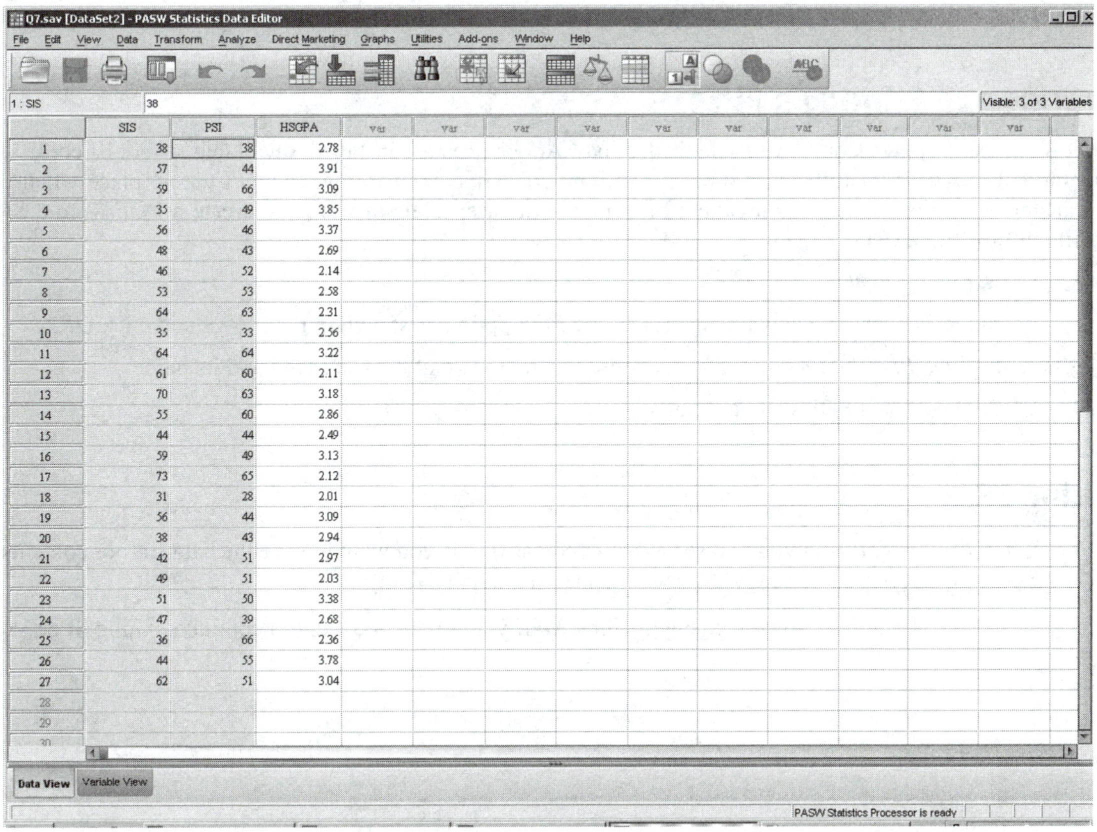

Figure 8.2 Selected variables for pasting.

Printing an SPSS Data File and Exiting SPSS

Printing an SPSS data file provides you a non-electronic copy of your data. Below we describe how to print an SPSS data file as well as create and print a PDF (portable document file) of the data file. We also describe how to exit SPSS.

Printing an SPSS Data File

Open the file you want to print. For example, you can open the data file used in the previous QuickStart, Q8.sav.

1. Click *File → Print*. You will see the *Print* dialog box as shown in Figure 9.1. *All* will be selected in the *Print Range* area. If you prefer to print only a portion of your data set, click and drag over the part of the data set you want printed prior to clicking *File → Print*. In this case, *Selection* will be selected in the *Print Range* area.

2. Click *OK*, and the file will be printed. The printed copy includes the name of the file, the data, and the time and date the file information was printed.

Creating and Printing a PDF

A PDF can be displayed on any machine that has Adobe Reader installed (available at adobe.com). The advantage of a PDF is it can be shared easily, with no concerns about format changes taking place when files are transferred. A disadvantage is it cannot be edited without special software. To create a PDF from a SPSS data file, follow these steps:

1. Click *File → Print*.
2. From the *Printer* drop down menu, select the *PDF* option as shown in Figure 9.2 and click *OK*.
3. In the *Save PDF File As* dialog box, choose where you want the file saved and its name.
4. Click *Save*, and a PDF will be created.

Exiting SPSS

1. Click *File → Exit*, and you will see a dialog box asking if you want to save the data file (or contents of the output viewer) if any changes were made to it and not saved.
2. Click *Yes*, if you want to save changes. Click *No* if you do not and want to continue exiting SPSS.

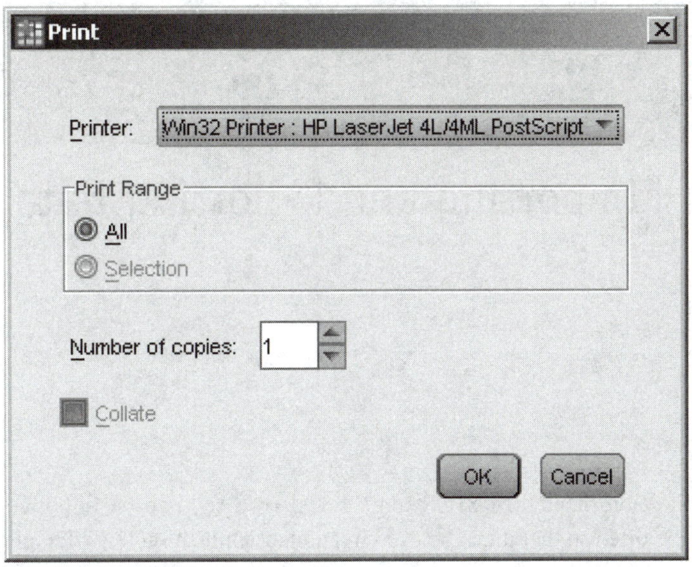

Figure 9.1 *Print* dialog box.

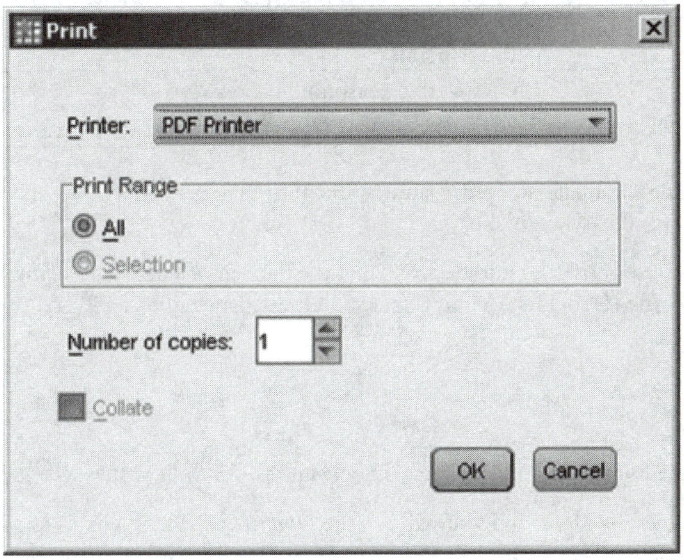

Figure 9.2 Selecting the PDF printer.

QuickStart 10   Importing and Exporting Data

Data created in an application other than SPSS (e.g., Excel or SAS) can be imported into SPSS. Also data created in SPSS can be exported so that it can be used in another application (e.g., Excel or SAS).

The Data

Our example data are in two files: an Excel file named Q10.xls and an SPSS data file named Q10-11.sav.

Variable	Description
Verbal	GRE verbal reasoning scores
Quantitative	GRE quantitative reasoning scores

The example data include Graduate Record Examination (GRE) scores in verbal and quantitative reasoning. With the example data, we illustrate how to

- Import an Excel file (Q10.xls) into SPSS so that the data can be analyzed using SPSS.
- Export an SPSS file (Q10-11.sav) into Excel so that the data can be analyzed or manipulated using Excel.

Importing Data

To import data stored in a non-SPSS data file (e.g., Excel) into SPSS, follow these steps.

1. Click *File → Open → Data*, and you will see the *Open Data* dialog box as shown in Figure 10.1.
2. Click on the drop down menu labeled *Files of type*, and choose the type of file that you wish to import. For our example, we want to import an Excel file so we click on *Excel (*.xls, *.xlsx, *.xlsm)*, as you can see in Figure 10.2.
3. Locate the specific file on your drive that you want to import into SPSS (e.g., Q10.xls) and click on it.
4. Click *Open*. For some types of files, including Excel files, you will see a dialog box specifically designed for these types of files. In most instances, it is safe to click *OK* in this dialog box. The data should now be imported into the SPSS *Data Editor*.
5. Save the data as an SPSS data file if you plan to use it in the future. See QuickStart 4 for how to save an SPSS data file.

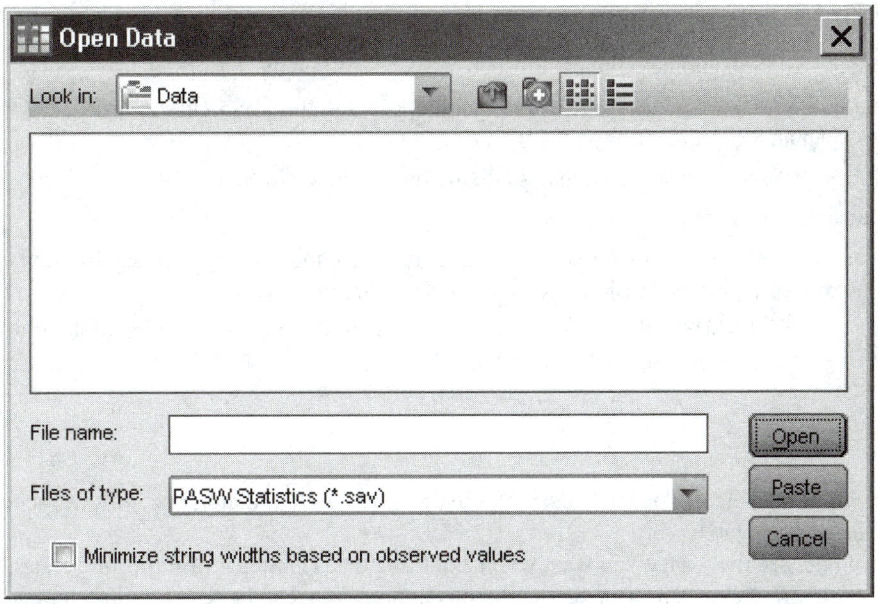

Figure 10.1 *Open Data* dialog box.

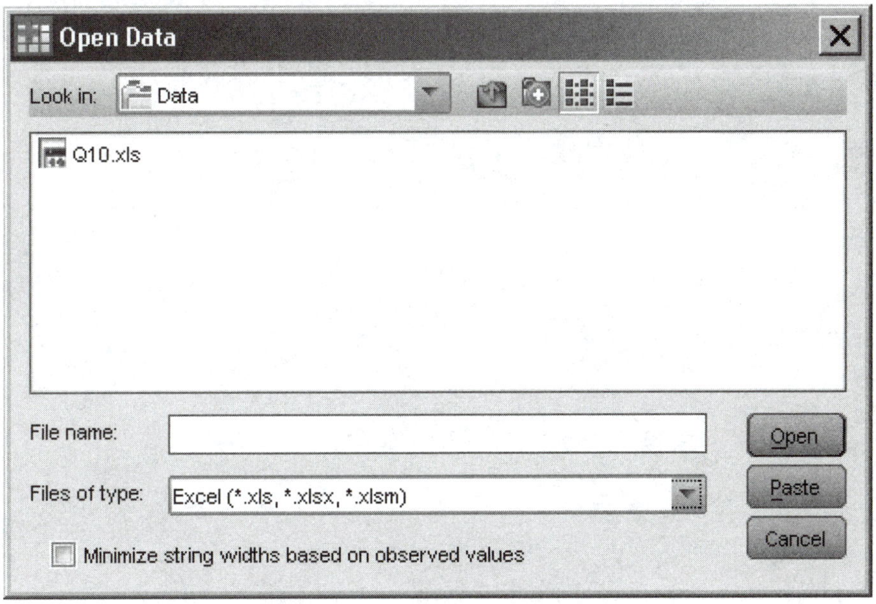

Figure 10.2 Drop down menu for selecting the type of file to open.

Exporting Data

To export data from SPSS to another application such as Excel, follow these steps.

1. Open the SPSS data (e.g., Q10-11.sav) so that it appears in the SPSS *Data Editor*. See QuickStart 4 for how to open an SPSS data file.

2. Click *File → Save As*. The *Save Data As* dialog box is shown in Figure 10.3.

3. Type a name for the new file.

4. Click on the drop down menu labeled *Save As Type*, and choose the type of file for your exported file. For our example, the type of file is *Excel 97 through 2003 (*.xls)*.

5. Click *Save*, and the SPSS file should be saved as the new file type. For our example, it was saved as an Excel file, which you can see in Figure 10.4.

More ...

- When exporting data, if you click *Variables* in the *Save As Data* dialog box, you can specify the variables you want to export.
- If you do not see the format you want when exporting data (in Step 4 of Exporting Data), save the file as *Fixed ASCII (*.dat)*. This is a very common data type that can be read by most applications.
- You can export an SPSS data set to a database (e.g., dBase, Excel and Access) by clicking on *File* from the main menu and choosing the *Export to Database* option.

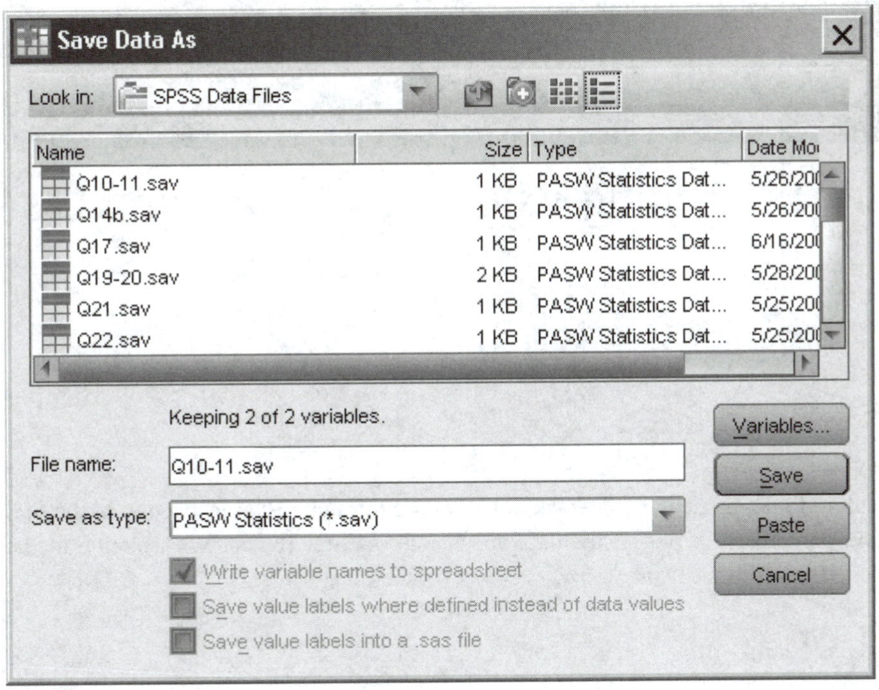

Figure 10.3 *Save As* dialog box.

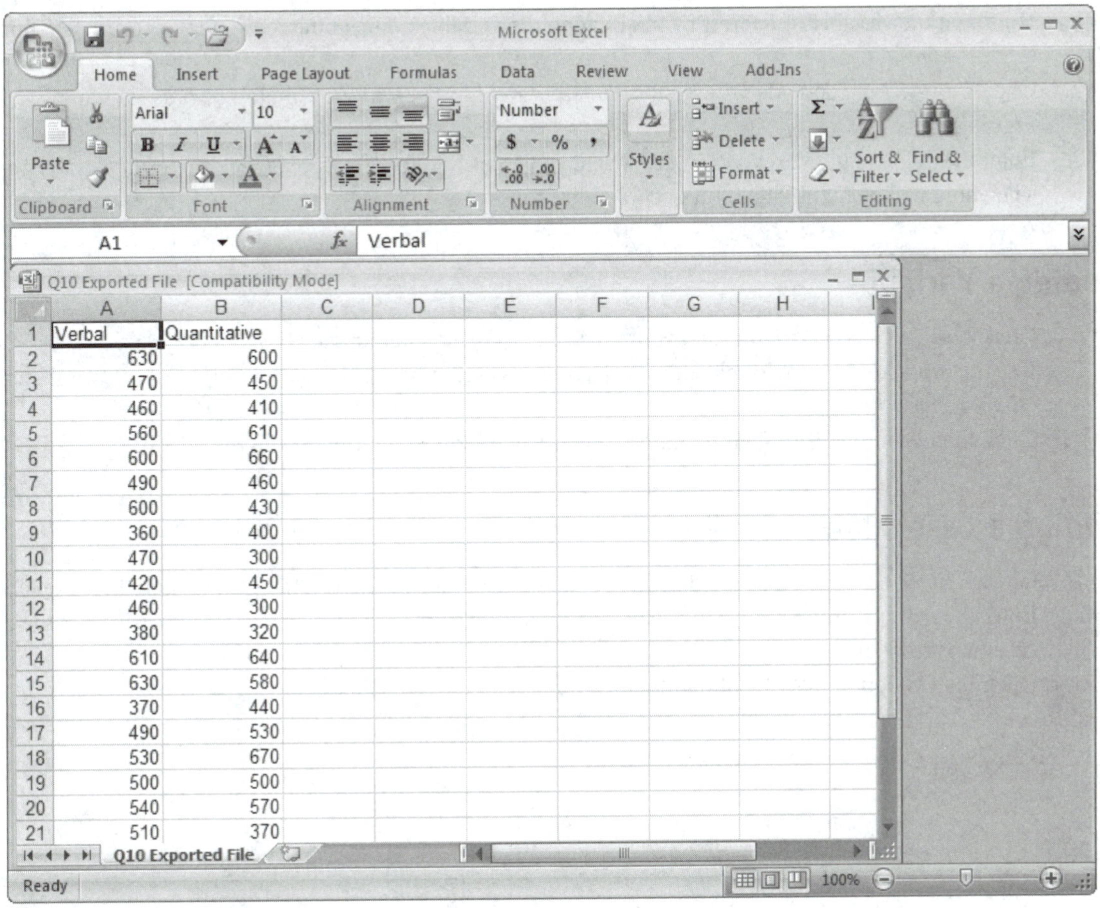

Figure 10.4 Exported Excel file.

QuickStart 11 | Finding Values, Variables, and Cases

It can be difficult to find a particular value, variable, or case through visual inspection in the SPSS *Data Editor* (*Data View* tab), particularly if not all the data are visible on your screen. We describe methods for finding values, variables, or cases in the *Data Editor*.

The Data

Our example data are in the file named Q10 – 11.sav, which was described in QuickStart 10.

Finding a Value for a Variable

1. Highlight the variable of interest by clicking on the variable name at the top of the appropriate column (e.g., *Verbal*).
2. Click *Edit → Find* and you will see the *Find and Replace – Data View* dialog box, as shown in Figure 11.1.
3. Enter the value (e.g., 380) you want to locate and enter it in the *Find* box. Click the *Find Next* button. The value will be highlighted if it occurs in the column.

Finding a Variable

1. Click *Edit → Go To Variable*, and you will see the *Variable* tab in the *Go To* dialog box.
2. Use the drop down menu to select the variable you want to find. As shown in Figure 11.2, we selected *Quantitative*.
3. Click the *Go* button. SPSS will highlight the variable (column) of interest in the data file.

Finding a Case (Row)

1. Click *Edit → Go To Case*, and you will see the *Case* tab in the *Go To* dialog box Click the Case tab.
2. Enter the number of the case (e.g., 23) you want to find in the *Go to case number* box (or click the up or down arrow buttons).
3. Click the *Go* button. SPSS will highlight the case (row) in the data file.

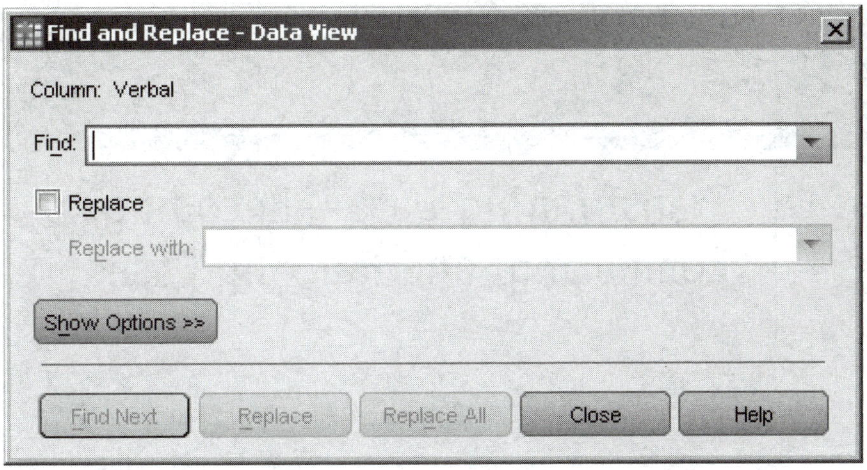

Figure 11.1 *Find and Replace - Data View* dialog box.

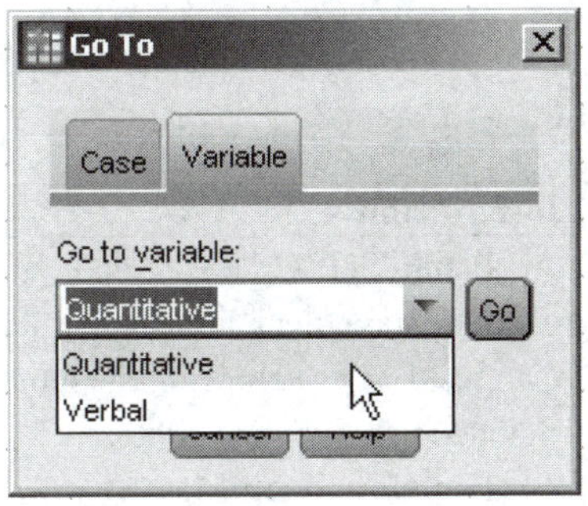

Figure 11.2 *Go To* dialog box.

Transforming Data—Recoding, Computing, and Ranking Cases

The scores on a variable may have to be transformed to conduct analyses of interest. We demonstrate transforming variables using the *Recode*, *Compute*, and *Ranking* commands.

The Data

Our example data are in the file named Q12-13.sav.

Variable	Description
ASCS	Academic Self-Concept Scale
Math	Math achievement subtest
Lang	Language Arts achievement subtest
Sc	Science achievement subtest
Gender	1 = Female and 2 = Male

With the example data, we illustrate *Recode*, *Compute*, and *Ranking* commands.

- *Recode* is used to transform Academic Self-Concept Scale (ASCS) scores with values from 1 to 75 to a recoded variable named ASCS_R with values from 1 to 3: 1 for low (ASCS scores between 1 and 25), 2 for medium (ASCS scores between 26 and 50), and 3 for high (ASCS scores between 51 and 75).

- *Compute* is used to calculate for each person a mean of scores on the math, language arts, and science subtests. These mean scores are stored in a newly created variable named m_Test.

- *Rank Cases* is used to create a new variable named Rm_Test, which contains the ranks associated with the scores for m_Test.

Recoding Scores for a New Variable

1. Click *Transform → Recode into Different Variables*, and you will see the *Recode into Different Variables* dialog box.

2. Double click the variable you want to transform (e.g., ASCS). Type in the name for the recoded variable (e.g., ASCS_R) in the *Name* box under *Output Variable*, and then click the *Change* button. The result of this step can be seen in Figure 12.1.

3. Click the *Old and New Values* button. You will now see the *Recode into Different Variables: Old and New Values* dialog box.

4. Click the *Range* button under *Old Value* and enter the range you want to include (e.g., 1 through 25). Type the new value (e.g., 1) in the *Value* box under *New Value*. Click the *Add* button (see Figure 12.2). Continue this process, entering the range under *Old Value*, the *Value* under *New Value*, and clicking the *Add* button.

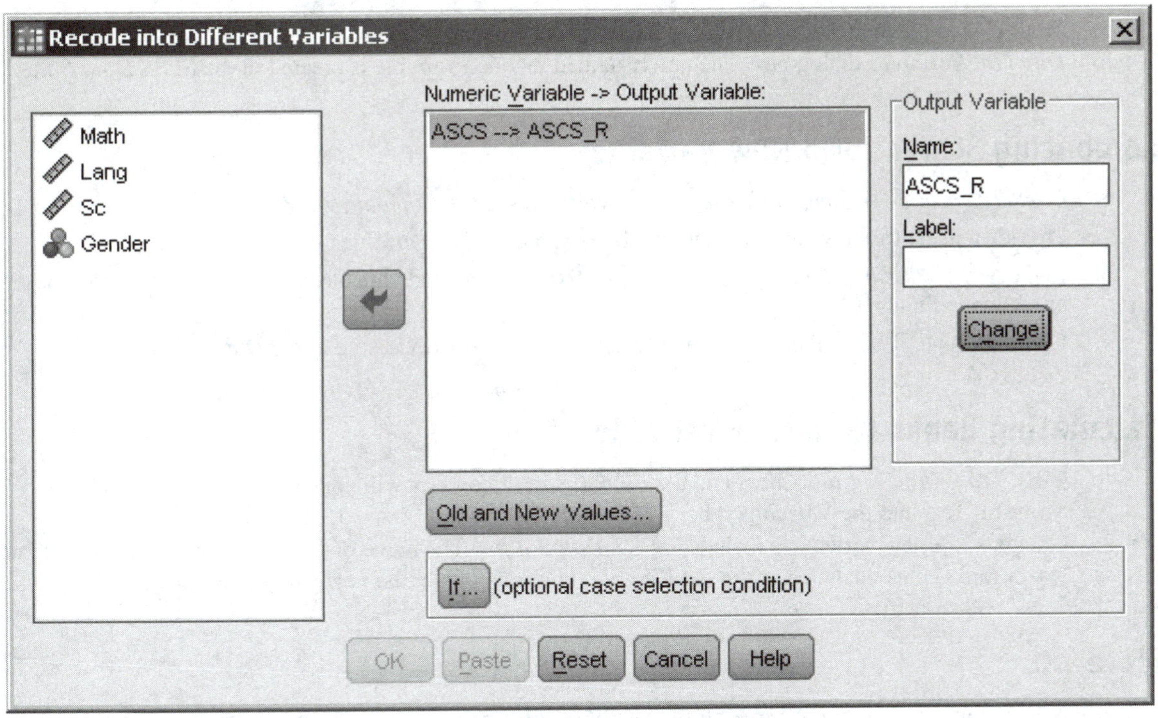

Figure 12.1 *Recode into Different Variables* dialog box.

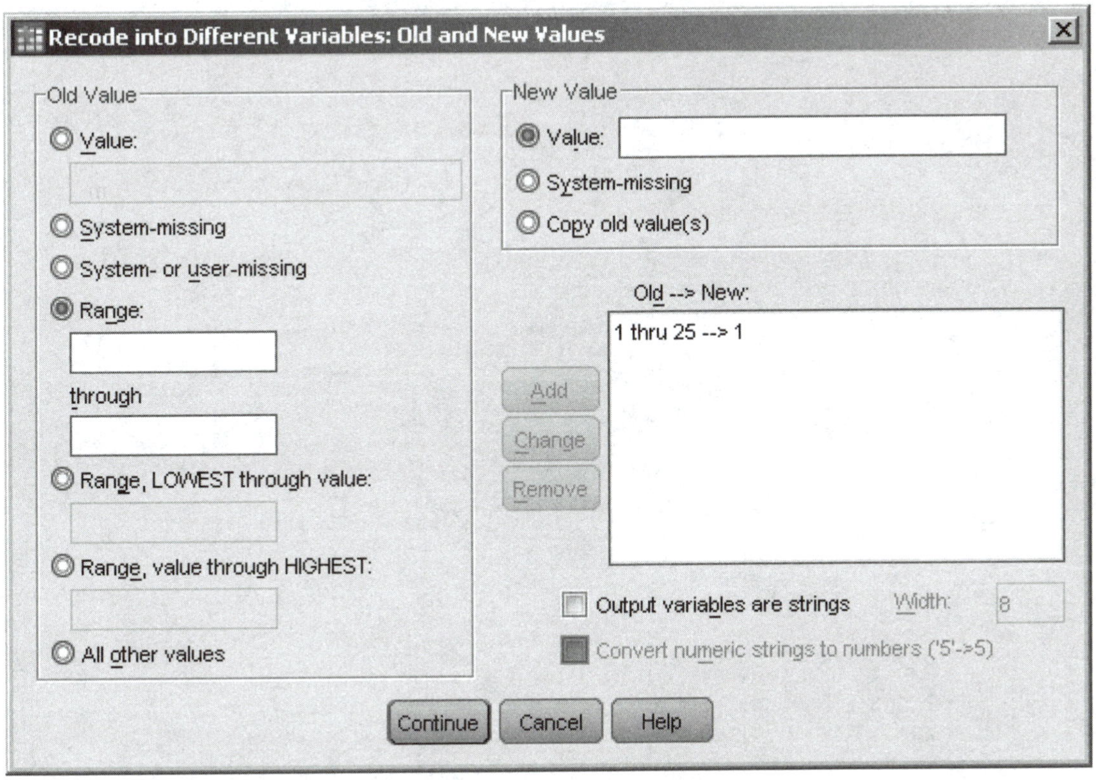

Figure 12.2 *Recode into Different Variables: Old and New Values* dialog box.

5. Press *Continue* when you have entered all recoded values and then click *OK* in the *Recode into Different Variables* dialog box. The newly named recoded variable is created in the SPSS *Data Editor*.

Computing Scores for a New Variable

1. Click *Transform → Compute Variable,* and you will see the *Compute Variable* dialog box.
2. Provide a name for new variable (e.g., m_Test) in the *Target Variable* box.
3. In the *Numeric Expression* box, enter a formula for the computed variable, such as (Math + Lang + Sc)/3, as shown in Figure 12.3.
4. Click *OK,* and SPSS will create the newly named transformed variable in the *Data Editor.*

Calculating Ranks for a New Variable

1. Click *Transform → Rank Cases* and the *Rank Cases* dialog box will appear.
2. Move m_Test into the *Variable(s)* box. The result is shown in Figure 12.4.
3. Click *OK.* A new variable is included in the *Data Editor.* The name of the new variable begins with an R (for ranks) plus the name of the old variable. In our example, the new variable is Rm_Test.

More ...

- In step 3 under *Computing Scores for a New Variable,* the m_Test score was computed using the formula (Mean + Lang + Sc)/3. If scores were missing in the data set, the m_Test score would be coded as missing if a score is missing for any variable in the formula.

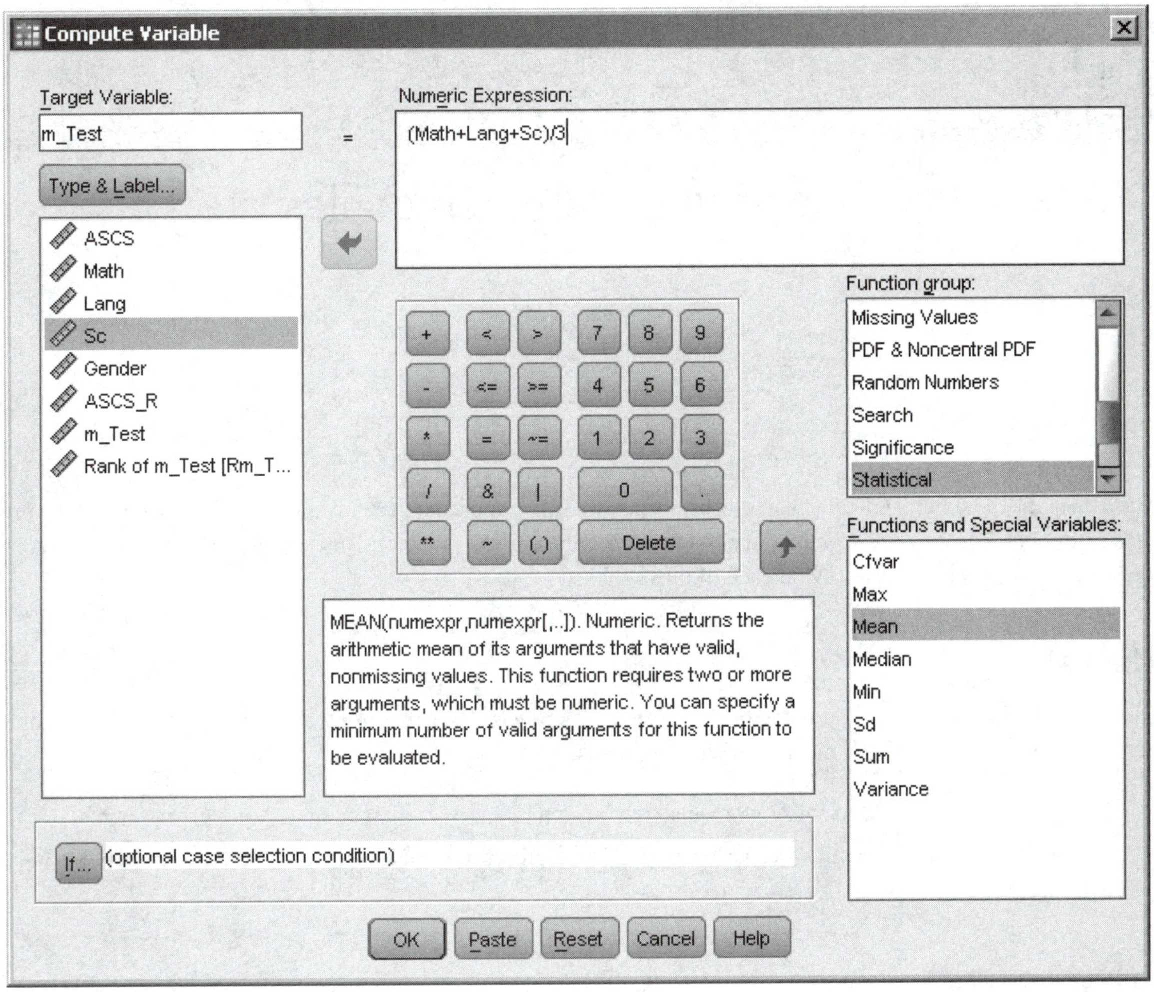

Figure 12.3 *Compute Variable* dialog box.

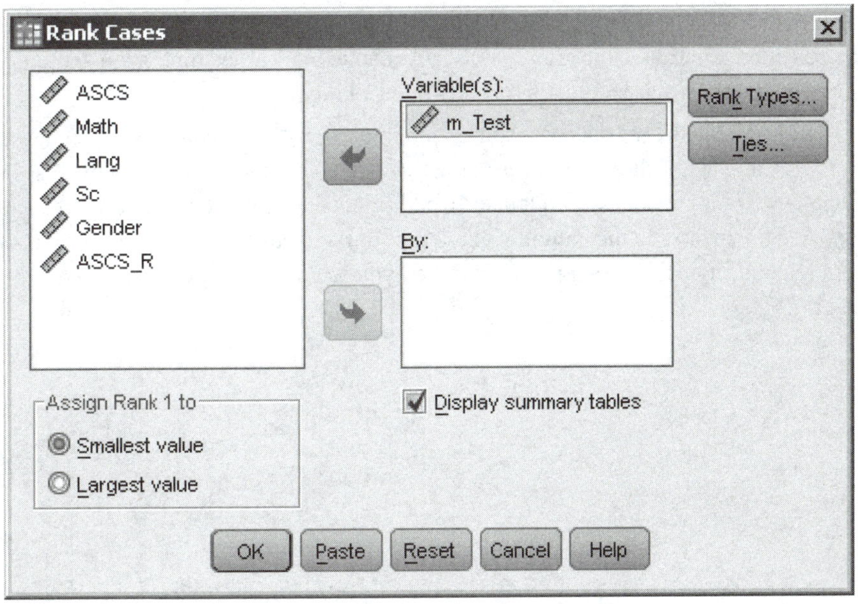

Figure 12.4 *Rank Cases* dialog box.

QuickStart 13 | Selecting and Splitting Files

The *Select Cases* command selects a subset of cases so that subsequent analyses are conducted on only this subset. In contrast, the *Split File* command splits the data into two or more subsets of data so that subsequent analyses are conducted separately on each of these subsets.

The Data

Our example data are in the file named Q12-13.sav, which was described in QuickStart 12. With the example data, we illustrate *Select Cases* and *Split File* commands.

- *Select Cases* is used to select women so that all future analyses are conducted on only women.
- *Split File* is used to split cases based on gender so all future analyses are conducted separately for men and women.

Selecting Cases

1. Click *Data → Select Cases*, and you will see the *Select Cases* dialog box shown in Figure 13.1.
2. Click the selection *If condition is satisfied*. Then click *If*.
3. Double click the variable that you want to use for making your selection of cases (e.g., Gender). Then type the selection criterion value after the variable name. For our example, you should type "= 1" to select females, as shown in Figure 13.2. Next click *Continue*.
4. Click *OK* in the *Select Cases* dialog box. The variable *filter_$* has been added as a new variable in the *Data Editor*. Cases with filter_$ = 1 (e.g., females) are included in subsequent analyses, while those with filter_$ = 0 (e.g., males) are excluded. In addition, the excluded cases have crossed-out case numbers. SPSS indicates in the bottom-right corner of the *Data Editor* that the filter is on. Whenever you want to conduct analyses on the total data set, you will have to click *Data → Select Cases → All cases → OK*.

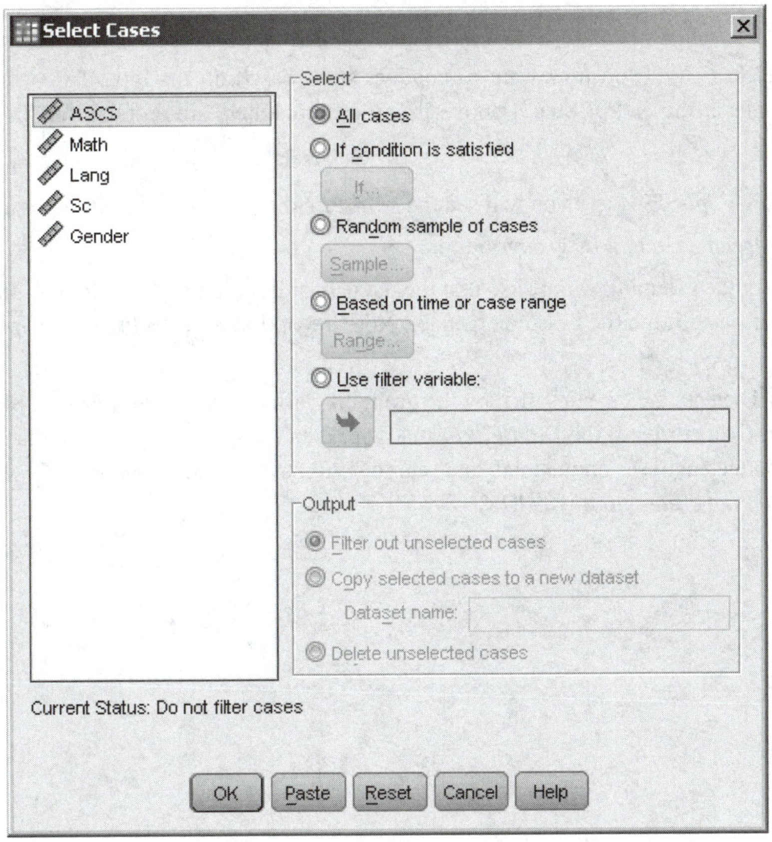

Figure 13.1 *Select Cases* dialog box.

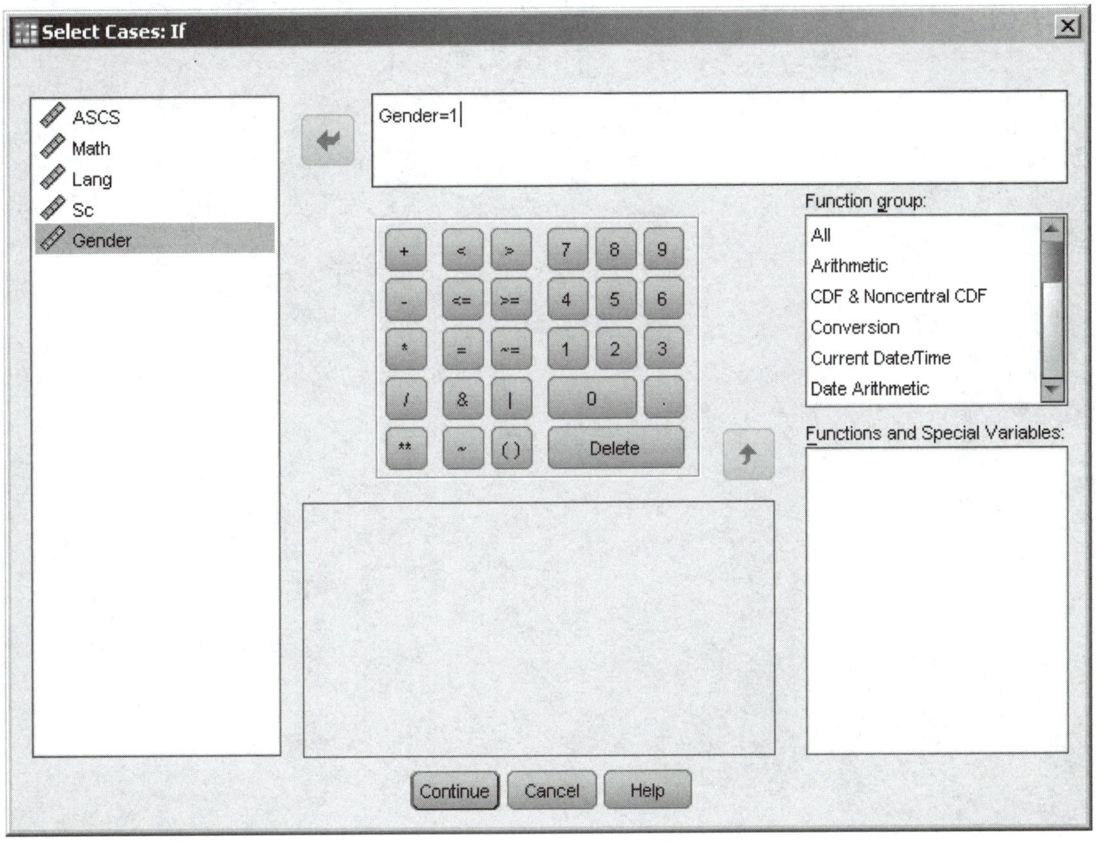

Figure 13.2 *Select Cases: If* dialog box.

Splitting a File

If you just used *Select Cases*, you now want to conduct steps based on the total data set. More specifically, follow the instructions at the end of Step 4 above if any case numbers are crossed out. To split a file, follow these steps:

1. Click *Data → Split File*, and you will see the *Split File* dialog box as shown in Figure 13.3.

2. Click the *Organize output by groups* button.

3. Double click the grouping variable so that the data are split based on this variable. In Figure 13.4 you can see that we split the file based on Gender. Note the option *Sort the file by grouping variables* is selected.

4. Click *OK*. The data have been sorted by the grouping variable in the *Data Editor*. SPSS indicates in the bottom-right corner of the *Data Editor* that your data are split (by gender in this example). If you want to conduct analyses on the total data set, you will have to choose *Data → Split File → Analyze all cases, do not create groups → OK*.

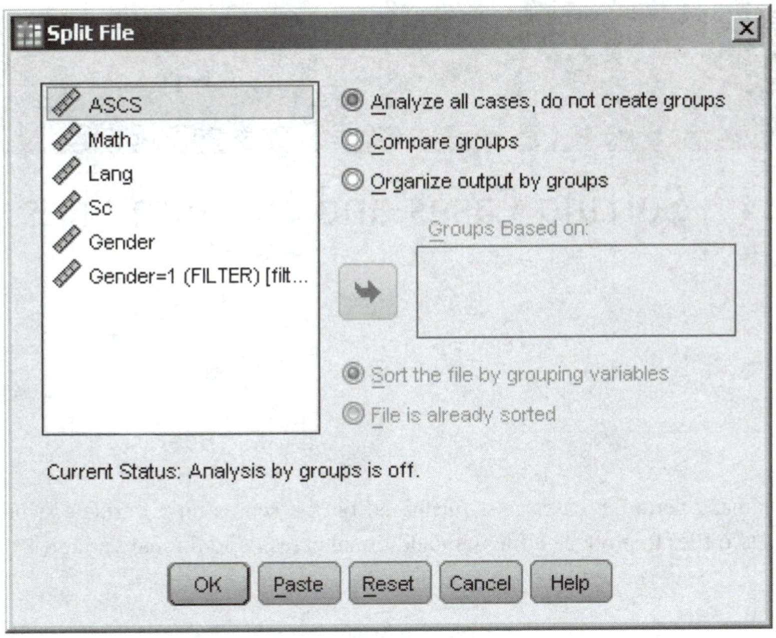

Figure 13.3 *Split File* dialog box.

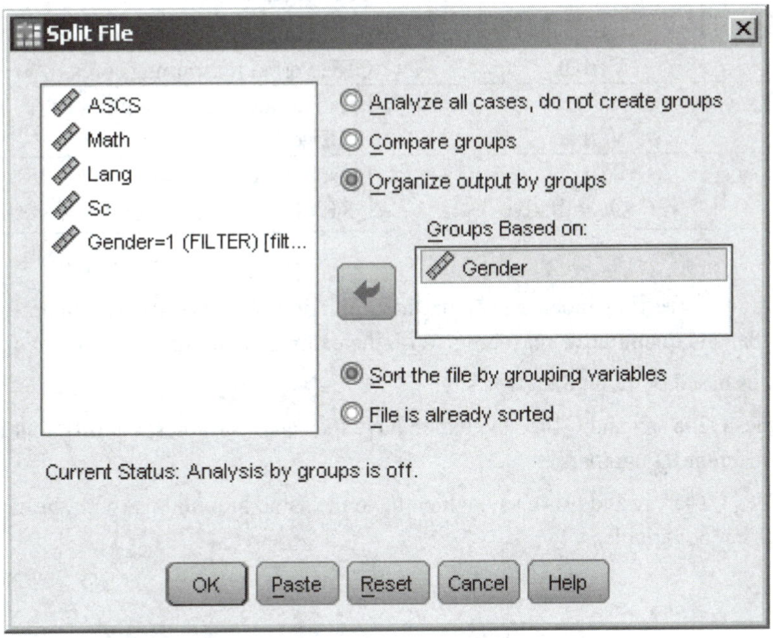

Figure 13.4 Splitting the data file based on Gender.

Sorting Cases and Merging Files

The *Sort Cases* command sorts the cases in a file based on the scores on a variable, while the *Merge Files* command combines two files to produce a file with additional cases or additional variables.

The Data

Our example data are in three files: Q14a.sav, Q14b.sav, and Q14c.sav.

File	Variable	Description
Q14a.sav	ID	Personal identification number
	Verbal	GRE verbal reasoning scores
Q14b.sav	ID	Personal identification number
	Verbal	GRE verbal reasoning scores
Q14c.sav	ID	Personal identification number
	Quantitative	GRE quantitative reasoning scores

The example data in the three files include personal identification numbers and Graduate Record Examination (GRE) scores in verbal and quantitative reasoning. With the example data, we illustrate the following:

- Sorting cases based on ID in the Q14a.sav.

- Merging files Q14a.sav and Q14b.sav, which have the same variables, but different individuals (with the different ID numbers).

- Merging files Q14a.sav and Q14c.sav, which have the same individuals (with the same ID numbers), but have different variables.

Sorting Data

1. Open an SPSS data file (e.g., 14a.sav).

2. Click *Data → Sort Cases*, and you will see the *Sort Cases* dialog box shown in Figure 14.1.

3. Double click on the variable (e.g., ID) that you want to sort by, and move it to the *Sort by* box. Click on *Ascending* or *Descending*. We clicked on *Ascending*.

4. Click *OK*. The data are now sorted in the *Data Editor* (e.g., from 1 to 20 on ID).

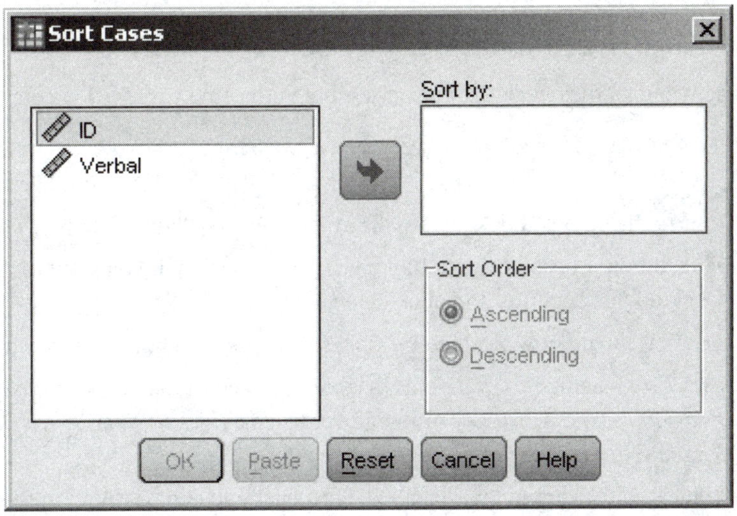

Figure 14.1 *Sort Cases* dialog box.

Merging Files with Different Cases, but Same Variables

We show how to merge two data files with different cases, but with some variables in common between them.

1. With one of the two files you want to merge open (e.g., 14a.sav), click *Data → Merge Files → Add Cases*.

2. In the *Add Cases to* dialog box, click next to *An external PASW Statistics data file*.

3. Click the *Browse* button. Locate the data file (e.g., Q14b.sav) which you want to merge with the file that is open. Click on this data file, and click *Open*.

4. Click *Continue*. You should now see the *Add Cases From* dialog box, as shown in Figure 14.2.

5. In the *Add Cases From* dialog box, variables that are not in common between the two files are listed in the *Unpaired Variables* box. Move any of them over to *Variables in New Active Dataset* box that you want in the merged file. There are none in our example.

6. Click *OK*. The merged data are in the file opened in step 1 and can be found in the *Data Editor*. We recommend that you save the file containing the merged data under a new name (*File → Save As*).

Merging Files with Different Variable, but Same Cases

We next demonstrate how to merge two data files with different variables, but with some cases in common between the two of them. We strongly advise that you include a common identification variable in both data sets (as we have done in our example datasets) and assume you have done so in the following steps:

1. Sort cases on the common identification variable in the two files you want to merge (e.g., sort by ID in Q14a.sav and Q14c.sav). Save the sorted files.

2. With one of the two files open (e.g., Q14a.sav), click *Data → Merge Files → Add Variables*, and you will see the *Add Variables to* dialog box.

3. In the *Add Variables to* dialog box, click the *Browse* button and locate the data file (e.g., Q14c.sav) that you want to merge with the file that is open. Click on this data file, and click *Open*.

4. Click *Continue*. The *Add Variables from* dialog box appears, as shown in Figure 14.3.

5. Click in the box next to *Match cases on key variables in sorted files* in the *Add Variables from* dialog box.

6. Click the variable in the *Excluded Variables* box that is the identification variable and is in common between the two datasets (e.g., ID). Move it to the *Key Variables* box.

7. Click *OK*. You will see a warning box. If you have sorted the files in step 1, there should be no problem. Click *OK*. The merged data are in the file opened in step 1 and can be found in the *Data Editor*. We recommend that you save the file containing the merged data under a new name (File → Save As).

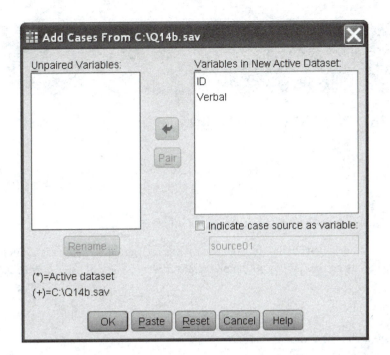

Figure 14.2 *Add Cases From* dialog box.

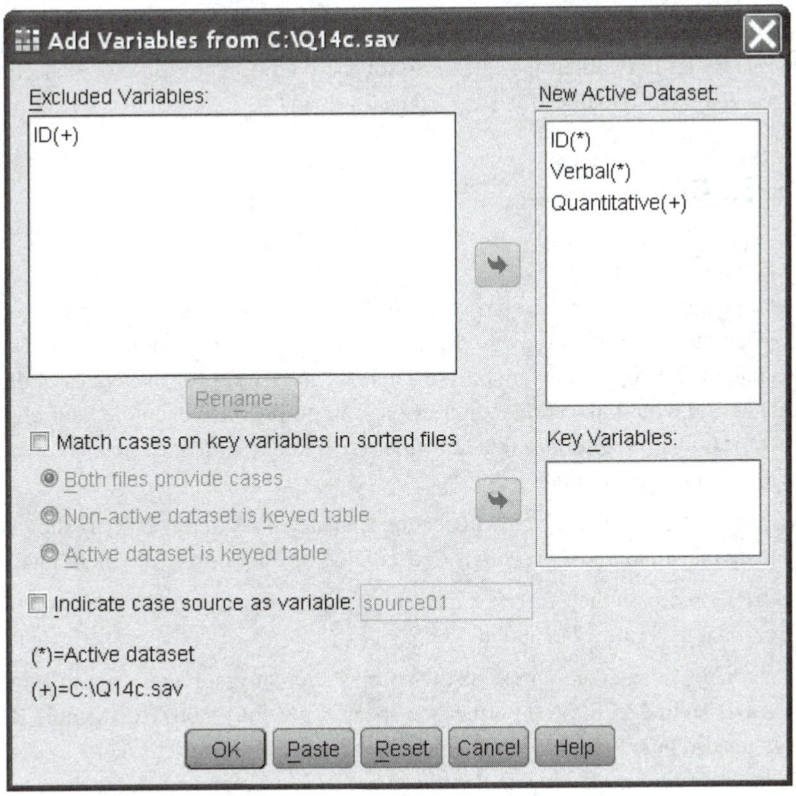

Figure 14.3 *Add Variables from* dialog box.

PART IV

Creating and Editing SPSS Graphs and Tables

Creating Graphs

A great way to develop an understanding of your data is through graphs. You have a number of methods for creating graphs in SPSS using the *Graphs* option on the *Main Menu*. We will use *Chart Builder*.

The Data

Our example data are in the file named Q15-16.sav.

Variable	Description
LikeStats	Responses to question about liking a statistics course.

For our example, a simple bar chart will be created for data obtained from 40 students taking a statistics course. The data are responses on an item about the likeability of the course. The response scale ranged from 1 to 5. The verbal anchors ranged from "Dislike" for 1 to "Like" for 5.

Creating an SPSS Graph

To create a graph, follow these steps:

1. Prior to creating a graph, ensure the properties of the variable(s) you will graph are appropriate. To do so, review your choices by clicking the *Variable View* tab at the bottom left in the *Data Editor*. Make changes so that the labels for the variables of interest (*Label*) and for the values of the variables (*Values*) are as you would like them to appear on your graph. Also examine your choice of measurement level within *Measure* (e.g., *Ordinal* for LikeStats); this choice has an effect on the options available in *Chart Builder*.

2. Click *Graphs → Chart Builder*. You will see the *Chart Builder* dialog box, as shown in Figure 15.1. (Prior to seeing this dialog box, you might see a dialog box about measurement level. Click *OK*.)

3. In the *Choose from* box in the *Gallery*, click on the general type of graph you want to create. For our example, we want to create a *Bar* graph.

4. Double click on the image that represents the specific type of graph you want to create. If you place your cursor over an image, SPSS describes the specific type of graph (e.g., Simple Bar). For our example, we placed our cursor over the Simple Bar graph, as shown in Figure 15.2, and then double clicked on it. After double clicking on the image, a preview graph appears in the Chart Builder dialog box.

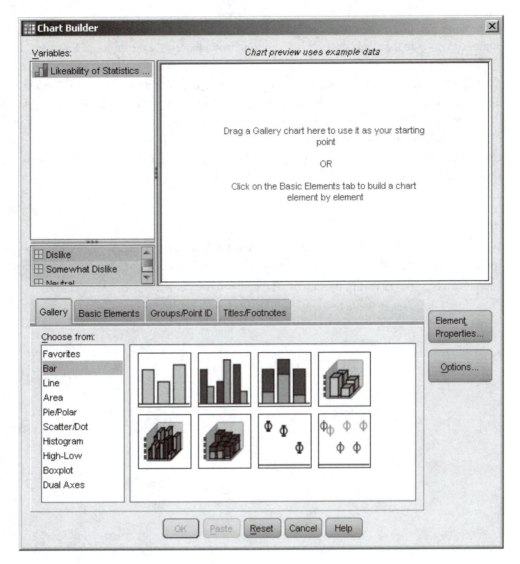

Figure 15.1 *Chart Builder* dialog box.

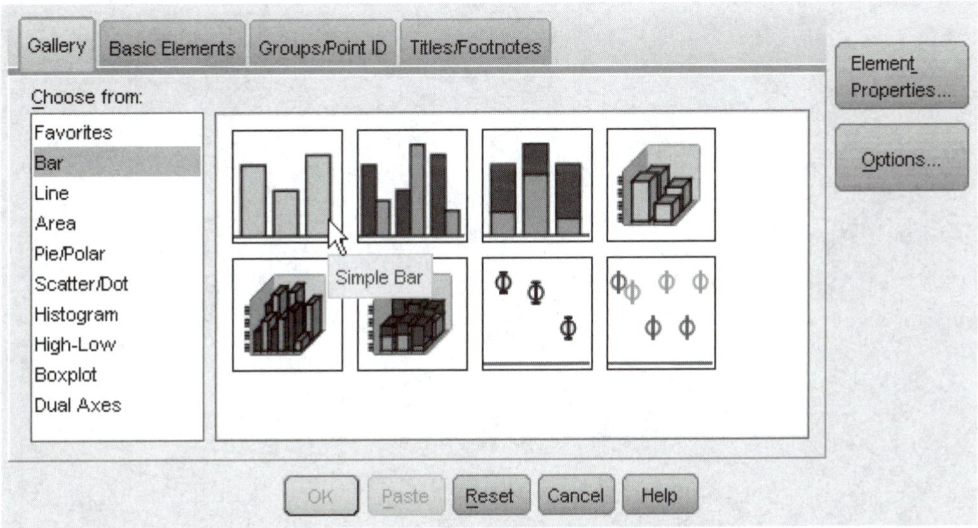

Figure 15.2 Selecting a specific type of graph.

5. In the upper half of the *Chart Builder* dialog box, drag the variable(s) in the *Variables* box to the appropriate axes in the *Chart preview* box. For our example, drag "Likeability of Statistics" in the *Variables* box to the *X-Axis*.

6. Click the *Element Properties* button. Edit properties of elements of the graph in the *Element Properties* dialog box. For our example, we edited the properties of the bars on the graph. Select *Bar1* in the *Edit Properties of* box, as shown in Figure 15.3. Then, select *Percentage (?)* in the *Statistic* drop down menu. Click *Apply* at the bottom of the *Element Properties* dialog box.

7. Click *OK* in the *Chart Builder* dialog box, and you will see the completed graph in the *Viewer*, as shown in Figure 15.4.

More ...

- We discussed only the *Gallery* tab in the *Chart Builder* dialog box. You can customize your graph further by choosing options in the *Basic Elements*, *Groups/Point ID*, and *Titles/Footnotes* tabs.

- Graphs can be saved as part of the output. The names of output files have *.spv* extensions.

- Once a chart is selected, it can be copied and pasted into any other application.

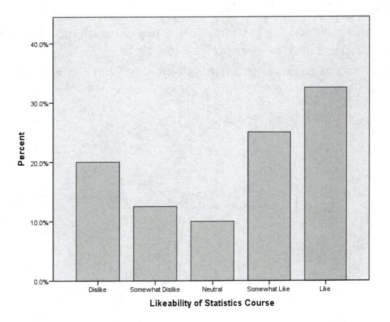

Figure 15.3 *Element Properties* dialog box.

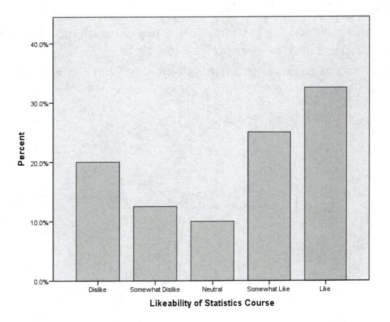

Figure 15.4 The completed chart in the *Viewer*.

Modifying Graphs

Almost any element in a graph can be modified in SPSS. It is appropriate to modify a graph to make it more readily understood by others. A general strategy for modifying most elements of graphs (exceptions include labels of axes) involves double clicking on the graph in the *SPSS Output Viewer* so that it appears in the *Chart Editor*. Then click on the element in the graph that you want to change (e.g., the bars in a simple bar graph), and choose among the possible changes in the pop-up *Properties* dialog box. The contents of the *Properties* dialog box vary as a function of the element that is selected for modification. After you click *Apply* in this box and exit the *Chart Editor*, the finished graph appears in *SPSS Output Viewer*.

The Data

Our example data are in the file named Q15-16.sav.

Variable	Description
LikeStats	Responses to question about liking a statistics course. Responses range from 1 (=dislike) to 5 (=like).

For our example, we illustrate the general strategy described above by making changes to the bars in the graph created in QuickStart 15. We also illustrate making changes to a label, specifically the label for the X axis.

Modifying Most Elements of a Graph

1. Double click on a graph in the *SPSS Statistics Viewer* (e.g., the graph created in QuickStart 15), and you will see the *Chart Editor*, as shown in Figure 16.1.

2. Double click on one of the bars in the graph displayed in the *Chart Editor*. You will see a *Properties* dialog box, as shown in Figure 16.2.

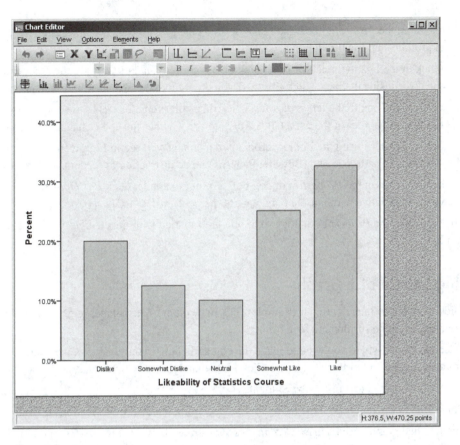

Figure 16.1 *Chart Editor*.

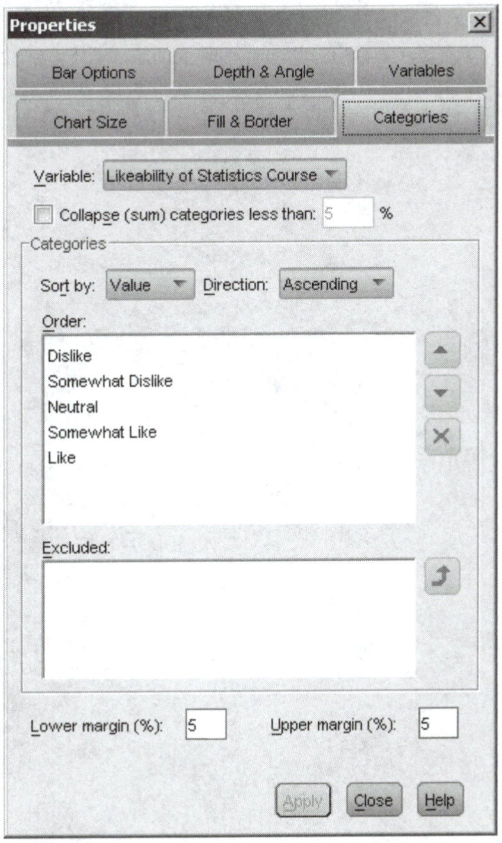

Figure 16.2 *Properties* dialog box for editing the bars.

3. Click a tab in the *Properties* box and make desired changes. For our example, click the *Fill & Border* tab and follow steps 3a through 3c:

   a. Click in the box to the left of *Fill*. Click on a color (e.g., a dark grey) in the color chart to change the color inside the bars. Click *Apply*. If you do not like the change, choose an alternative color.

   b. Click in the box to the left of *Border*. Click on a color (e.g., black) in the color chart to change the color of the border of the bars. Click *Apply* to see whether the color change is satisfactory.

   c. Select a pattern from the *Pattern* drop down menu, as you see in Figure 16.3. Click *Apply* to see whether the pattern is ok. (Beware: Patterns can be distracting to readers. We chose no pattern.)

4. Click another tab in the *Properties* dialog box. For our example, click *Bar Options*. Move the slide bar to change the relative width of the bars (e.g., 60 percent). Click *Apply*.

5. Click *Close* in the *Properties* dialog box if you are satisfied with the changes you have made to the graph.

Modifying Labels of a Graph

1. Click the label of interest. In our example, click once on the X-axis label (e.g., Likeability of Statistics Course). It will be surrounded by a frame.

2. Place the cursor where you want to make the edit and click. In our example, we want to add "by Students" at the end of the label so we click immediately after "Course."

3. Type in the desired text (e.g., " by Students").

4. Click *File → Close* in the *Chart Editor* if you have completed all modifications to your graph.

5. The finished graph appears in *SPSS Statistics Viewer*, as shown in Figure 16.4. You might save the graph or copy and paste it into another application, such as a word processor or a database.

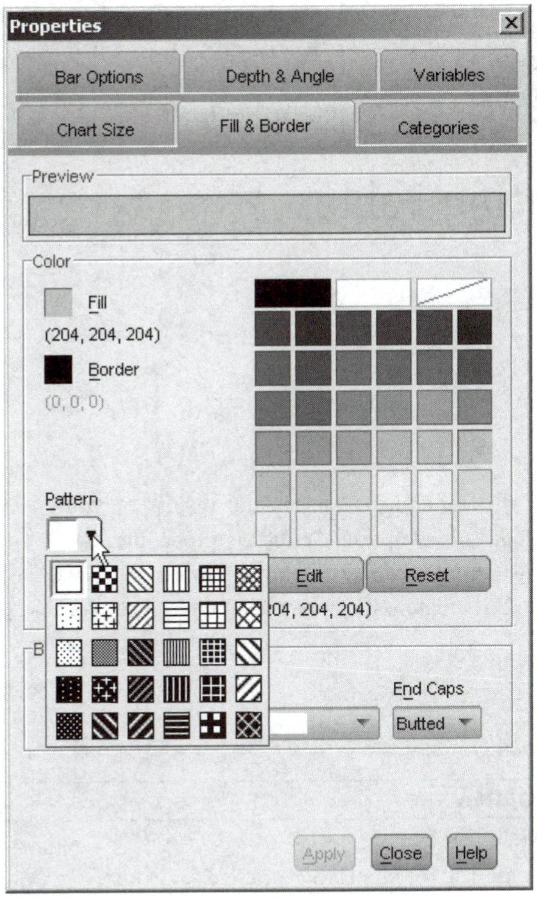

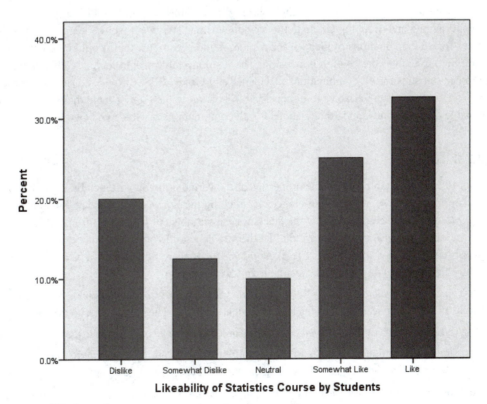

Figure 16.3 *Pattern* drop down menu.

Figure 16.4 Modified graph.

QuickStart 17 | Creating Tables

A well-designed table allows you to communicate clearly the results of your data. You can create a wide assortment of tables using the *Custom Tables* option. With this procedure, SPSS anticipates the type of table you want to create based on the measurement scale (i.e., nominal, ordinal, or scale) of the variables you choose to include in your table. Once the table is created, it can be modified to meet your needs.

The Data

Our example data are in the file named Q17.sav.

Variable	Description
Gender	1 = Male, 2 = Female
Grade	1 = grade 1, 2 = grade 2, 3 = grade 3
Self_Esteem	Scores on a self-esteem scale

With the example data, we could construct a variety of tables. We could create a table of frequencies for each gender by dragging and dropping Gender to the column dimension. We could build a more complex table by adding a step: dragging and dropping Grade to the row dimension. The result would be a two-dimensional table of frequencies for all combinations of Gender and Grade. A more complex table could be created by dragging and dropping Self-Esteem to the column dimension. The resulting table would include Self-Esteem means and potentially other statistics for all combinations of Gender and Grade. SPSS provides a visual representation of the table as you drag and drop variables to dimensions so you know the type of table that will be created. Here we create a table of means and standard deviations for all combinations of Grade and Gender.

Creating a Table

1. Prior to creating a table, ensure the properties of the variable(s) you will include in your table are appropriate. To do so, review your choices by clicking the *Variable View* tab at the bottom-left in the *Data Editor*. Make changes so that the labels for the variables of interest (*Label*) and for the values of the variables (*Values*) are as you would like them to appear in your table. Also examine your choice of measurement level within *Measure* (e.g., *Nominal* for Gender and *Ordinal* for Grade) in that this choice has an effect on the options available in *Custom Tables*.

2. Click *Analyze → Tables → Custom Tables*, and you will see the *Custom Tables* dialog box as shown in Figure 17.1. (Prior to seeing this dialog box, you might see a dialog box about measurement level. Click *OK*.)

3. Drag and drop a variable to the *Columns* or *Rows* dimension of the table (e.g., *Gender* to the *Columns* dimension).

4. Drag and drop additional variables to the appropriate dimensions (e.g., *Grade* to the *Rows* dimension and *Self_Esteem* to the *Columns* dimension), if necessary.

5. Click on the *Summary Statistics* button, if changes need to be made to statistics provided in the table. Drag the desired statistic (e.g., *Std. Deviation*) to the *Display* area. Click *Apply Selection*.

6. Click *OK* and see the completed table in the *Results* pane of the *Viewer* as shown in Figure 17.2.

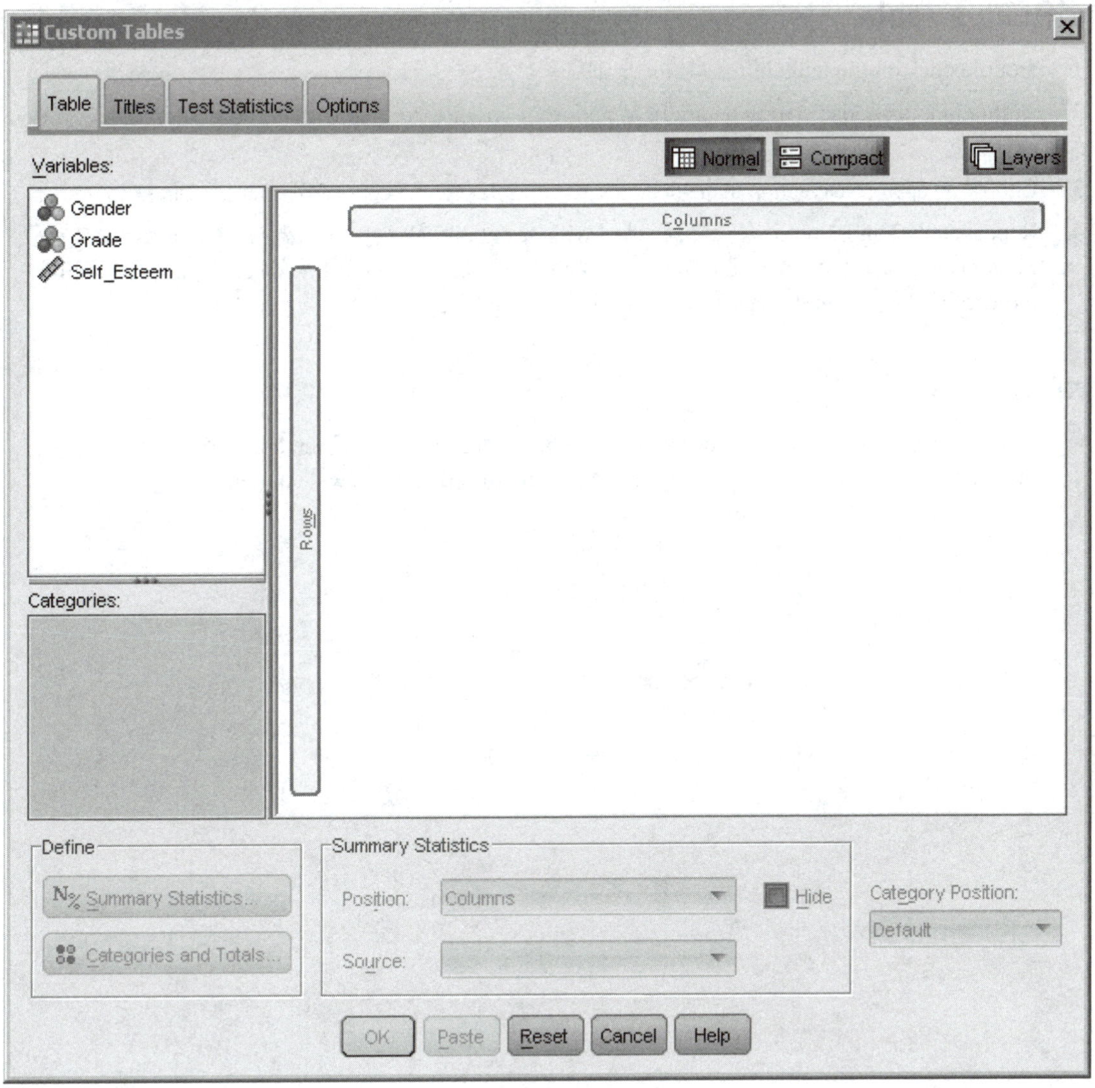

Figure 17.1 *Custom Tables* dialog box.

		Self_Esteem			
		Gender			
		Male		Female	
		Mean	Standard Deviation	Mean	Standard Deviation
Grade	1	61	12	61	12
	2	59	14	56	9
	3	53	11	57	8

Figure 17.2 Completed table using *Custom Tables*.

Modifying a Table

1. Double click on the table in the *Results* pane.

2. Right click to choose among a variety of options to modify your table. We chose *Table Looks* for our example.

3. Choose an appropriate option in the dialog box and click *OK*. We chose *CompactAcademicTimeRoman*.

4. Repeat steps 2 and 3 until you are satisfied with your table. We chose *Tables Properties → Cell Formats* and selected the centering icon in the *Alignment* area. You should see the newly modified table in the *Viewer* as shown in Figure 17.3.

More ...

- You can easily incorporate tables into other applications by selecting them in SPSS and then pasting them into the target document. They can then be modified in the new document.

		Self_Esteem			
		Gender			
		Male		Female	
		Mean		Mean	Standard Deviation
Grade	1	61	12	61	12
	2	59	14	56	9
	3	53	11	57	8

Figure 17.3 Modified table.

QuickStart 18 | Using the Viewer

The *Viewer* window contains the output from SPSS analyses (i.e., tables and graphs, as shown in Figure 18.1). On the left is the *Outline* pane, which lists the analyses that were completed. On the right is the *Contents* pane, which contains the actual results of analyses. You can click on an element in the *Outline* pane to go to that result in the *Contents* pane. Here we illustrate that you also can hide (or show), delete, or move results in the *Contents* pane by manipulating elements in the *Outline* pane. Be sure that when you click on the names of procedures in the *Output* window, you click on the icon representing the procedure and not the procedure name.

Example Viewer File

The *Viewer* file named Q18.spv (as you see in Figure 18.1) contains a table and a graph. To open a *Viewer* file, conduct the following steps:

1. Click *File → Open → Output* from the *Main Menu*.
2. Click on the file of interest (e.g., Q18.spv) in the folder where it is stored. All *Viewer* files have the appended name of *.spv*.

Hiding and Showing Results in the Contents Pane

1. Click on the icon next to the element of interest in the *Outline* pane of the *Viewer*.
2. Click *View → Hide* or click *View → Show* to hide or reveal the element in the *Contents* pane. As you see in Figure 18.2, we hid the table in the *Contents* pane, although it is available in the *Outline* pane.

Deleting Results in the Contents Pane

1. Click on the icon next to the element of interest in the *Outline* pane of the *Viewer*.
2. Click *Edit → Delete* to delete this element in the *Contents* pane.

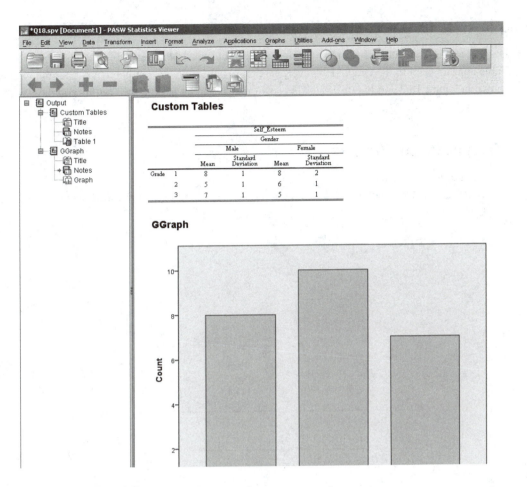

Figure 18.1 SPSS *Viewer* Window.

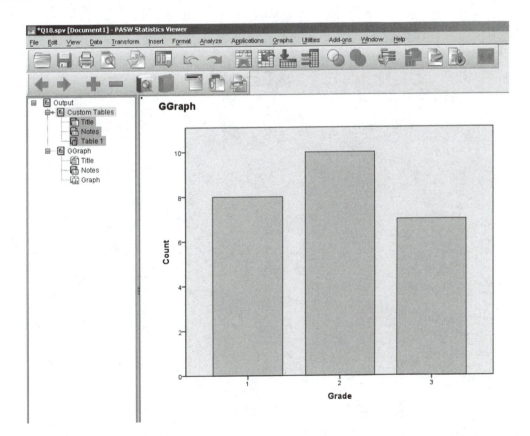

Figure 18.2 Hiding output in the *Contents* pane.

Moving Results in the Contents Pane

1. Drag an icon to a new location in the *Outline* pane. In our example seen in Figure 18.1, the Custom Table appears prior to the Graph. However, we dragged the table so that it appears after the graph, as shown in Figure 18.3 and Figure 18.4. This new order is shown in both the *Outline* and the *Contents* panes.

Saving Output in the Viewer

1. Click *File → Save as.*
2. Enter a name for the output. Note that the output is saved with the appended name of *.spv.*
3. Click *OK.*

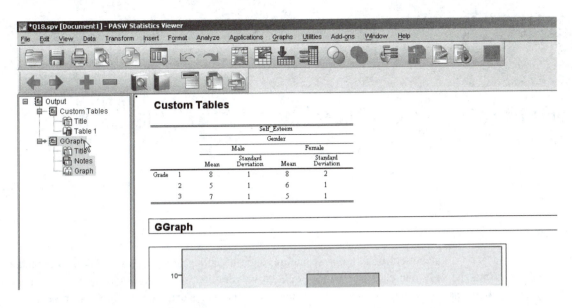

Figure 18.3 Dragging output elements.

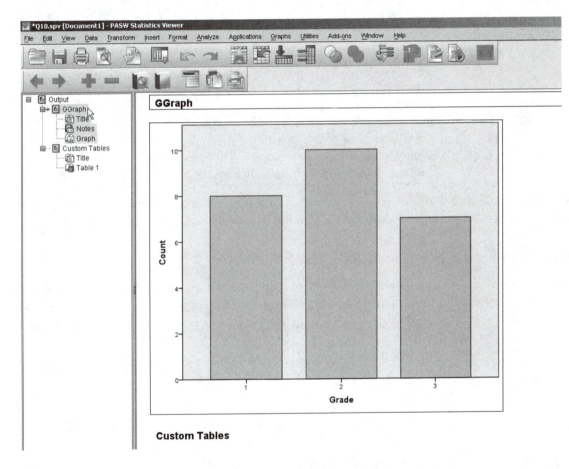

Figure 18.4 New ordering: GGraph prior to the Custom Tables.

PART V | Descriptive Statistics

QuickStart 19 | Descriptive Statistics for Qualitative Variables

Qualitative variables are categorical or nominal in nature, such as college major. Any individual should be classifiable into one and only one category using a qualitative variable. We demonstrate how to compute a mode, produce a frequency table, and create graphs for qualitative variables using the *Frequencies* procedure.

The Data

Our example data are in the SPSS data file named Q19-20.sav.

Variable	Description
Age	Age in years
Year	Year in school
Major	Name of major
ACT	ACT score
GPA	Cumulative grade point average
Ex_Curr	Type of extracurricular activities: 1 = Intramural sports, 2 = fraternity/sorority, 3 = community service, 4 = academic club

Frequencies can be used to describe the results on variables with a limited number of categories. We will examine the categorical variables of Major and Ex_Curr and the ordered categorical variable of Year.

Computing Frequencies for Qualitative Variables

1. Click *Analyze → Descriptive Statistics → Frequencies*, and you will see the *Frequencies* dialog box as shown in Figure 19.1. Note that, by default, the box next to *Display frequency tables* is checked.

2. Double click on the variables of interest to move them to the *Variable(s)* box. For our example, the variables are Major, Year, and Ex_Curr.

3. Click the *Statistics* button and click *Mode* in the *Central Tendency* box. The mode is the appropriate measure of central tendency for a categorical variable.

4. Click *Continue*.

5. Click *OK* and the Frequencies results will be in the output window, as shown in Figure 19.2.

Important Output and What It Means

- The frequencies and percents for the various categories are presented in each table. Because there are no missing data, the percents are identical to the valid percents, which are based on only those cases with the non-missing data on a variable.

- Note that the mode is the most frequently occurring category for a variable.

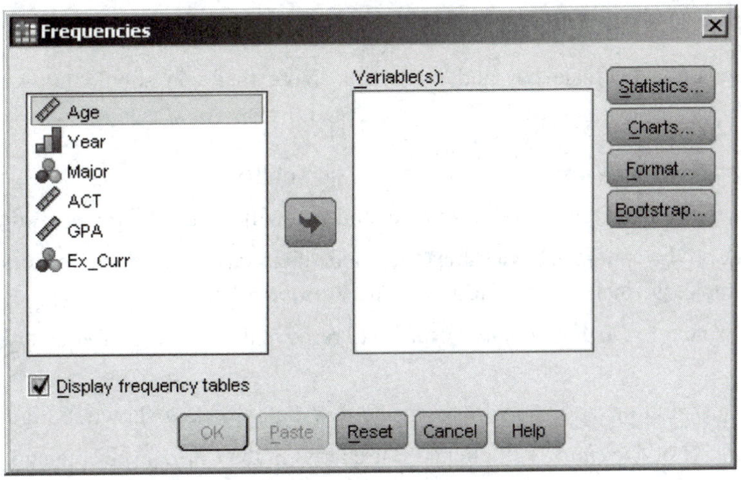

Figure 19.1 *Frequencies* dialog box.

Frequency Table

Major

		Frequency	Percent	Valid Percent	Cumulative Percent
Valid	Psychology	1	4.0	4.0	4.0
	Business	5	20.0	20.0	24.0
	Engineering	7	28.0	28.0	52.0
	Arts	8	32.0	32.0	84.0
	Journalism	3	12.0	12.0	96.0
	Other	1	4.0	4.0	100.0
	Total	25	100.0	100.0	

Year

		Frequency	Percent	Valid Percent	Cumulative Percent
Valid	First Year	8	32.0	32.0	32.0
	Second Year	7	28.0	28.0	60.0
	Third Year	4	16.0	16.0	76.0
	Fourth Year	6	24.0	24.0	100.0
	Total	25	100.0	100.0	

Ex_Curr

		Frequency	Percent	Valid Percent	Cumulative Percent
Valid	Intramural Sports	1	4.0	4.0	4.0
	Fraternity/Sorority	9	36.0	36.0	40.0
	Community Service	9	36.0	36.0	76.0
	Academic Club	6	24.0	24.0	100.0
	Total	25	100.0	100.0	

Figure 19.2 Results of analyses using *Frequencies*.

Creating Graphs Using *Frequencies*

We next demonstrate how to create bar and pie charts. Note that you should not create a histogram for qualitative variables.

1. Click the *Recall recently used dialogs* button on the Toolbar.

2. Click *Frequencies* from the drop down menu, and you will see the *Frequencies* dialog box.

3. Double click on the appropriate variables to include them or to exclude them from the *Variable(s)* box. For our example, we included only Major in the *Variable(s)* box.

4. Click the box next to *Display frequency tables* to remove the check if a frequency table is not necessary.

5. Click the *Charts* button, and you will see the *Charts* dialog box, as shown in Figure 19.3.

6. Click *Bar charts* or *Pie charts* (we clicked Bar charts) in the *Chart Type* area and then click *Continue*.

7. Click *OK*, and you will see the chart you selected in step 6. We show the bar chart in Figure 19.4. You can edit this as we showed you earlier in QuickStart 16.

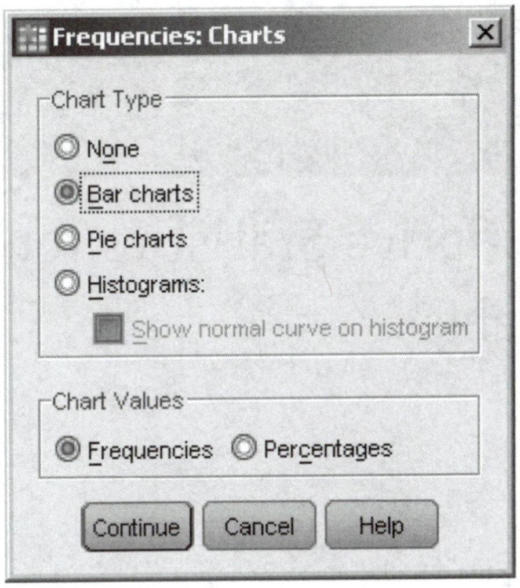

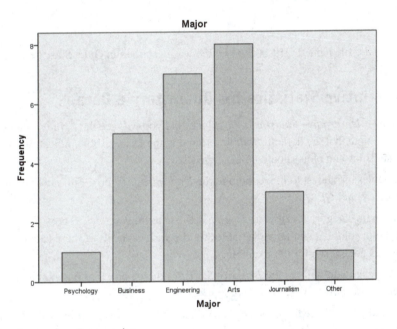

Figure 19.3 *Charts* dialog box.

Figure 19.4 Bar chart using *Frequencies*.

QuickStart 20 | Descriptive Statistics for Quantitative Variables

A variable is quantitative and represents a scale (an SPSS term) if the distance between values of a variable has quantitative meaning. These variables are measured at the interval or ratio level. We demonstrate how to compute descriptive statistics and to create a histogram for quantitative variables using the *Explore* option.

The Data

Our example data are in the file named Q19-20.sav, which was described in QuickStart 19.

Computing Descriptive Statistics for Quantitative Data

1. Click *Analyze → Descriptive Statistics → Explore,* and you will see the *Explore* dialog box as shown in Figure 20.1. Note that, by default, *Both* is selected in the *Display* box, indicating that both descriptive statistics and plots should be generated.

2. Drag the variables of interest to move them to the *Dependent List* box. For our example, we selected the variables *ACT* and *GPA.*

3. Move one or more categorical variables (e.g., *Ex_Curr*) to the *Factor List* box, if you want descriptive statistics and plots of the quantitative variables for the various levels of these categorical variables. This option was not chosen for our example.

4. Click *Statistics*, and you will see the *Explore: Statistics* dialog box. For our example, we chose the default option *Descriptives.* Click *Continue.*

5. Click *Plots*, and you will see the *Explore: Plots* dialog box as shown in Figure 20.2. Choose the desired plot. For our example, we unchecked *Stem-and-leaf* and checked *Histogram* in the *Descriptive* box. We chose *None* under *Boxplots.* Click *Continue.*

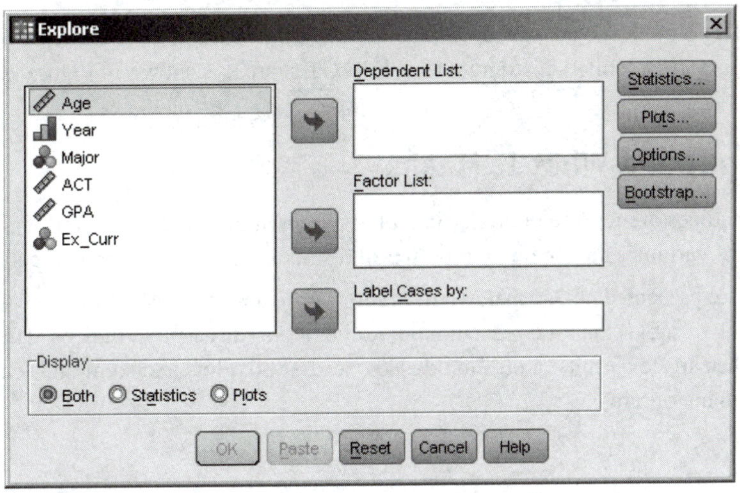

Figure 20.1 *Explore* dialog box.

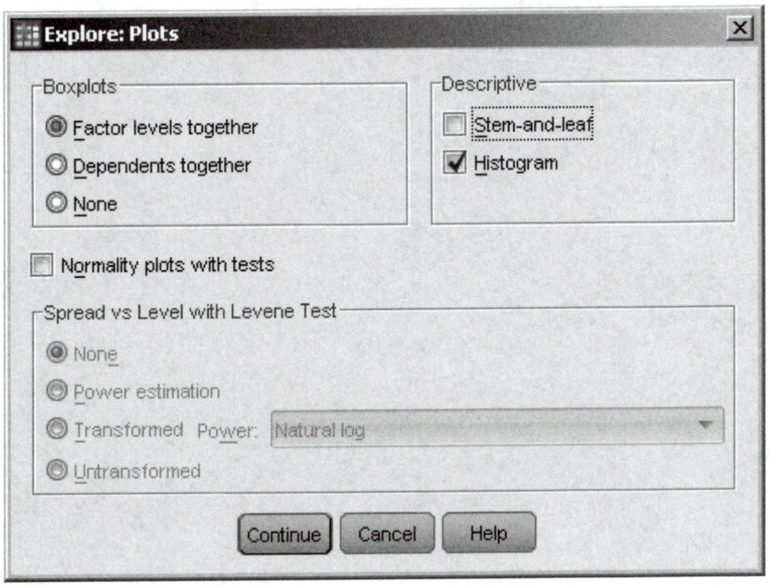

Figure 20.2 *Explore: Plots* dialog box.

6. Click *OK*, and you will see the partial results in the *Output* window. The descriptive statistics are shown in Figure 20.3, while a histogram (for the ACT scores) is shown in Figure 20.4.

Important Output and What It Means

- Descriptive indices are reported initially in tables shown in Figure 20.3. Means and standard deviations of quantitative variables are routinely reported in results sections of research papers.

- Histograms are presented next, as shown in Figure 20.4 These graphs are more descriptive of the distribution of variables than the presentation of one or two descriptive indices. They should be presented when space permits. You should also consider boxplots and stem-and-leaf plots as alternatives to histograms.

Descriptives

			Statistic	Std. Error
ACT	Mean		25.68	1.052
	95% Confidence Interval for Mean	Lower Bound	23.51	
		Upper Bound	27.85	
	5% Trimmed Mean		25.60	
	Median		26.00	
	Variance		27.643	
	Std. Deviation		5.258	
	Minimum		18	
	Maximum		35	
	Range		17	
	Interquartile Range		10	
	Skewness		.131	.464
	Kurtosis		-1.007	.902
GPA	Mean		2.9560	.11016
	95% Confidence Interval for Mean	Lower Bound	2.7286	
		Upper Bound	3.1834	
	5% Trimmed Mean		2.9700	
	Median		2.9000	
	Variance		.303	
	Std. Deviation		.55082	
	Minimum		1.80	
	Maximum		3.80	
	Range		2.00	
	Interquartile Range		.90	
	Skewness		-.230	.464
	Kurtosis		-.673	.902

Figure 20.3　Results of the descriptive statistics using *Explore*.

ACT

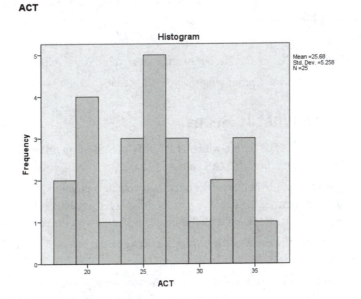

Figure 20.4　Histogram results using *Explore*.

One-Sample *t* Test

A one-sample *t* test assesses whether the population mean of a variable is different from a constant, which SPSS calls a test value. The constant is defined by the user to best address the research question.

The Data

Our example data are in the file named Q21.sav.

Variable	Description
CCAS	Climate Change Attitude Scale scores

In our example, a researcher wants to evaluate whether students believe climate change is more a function of natural fluctuations in weather or due to effects caused by people. Thirty students are assessed on the Climate Change Attitude Scale, which yields scores that range from 0 (due solely to natural fluctuations in weather) to 100 (due solely to human interventions). A score of 50 is the test value and represents an equal contribution of the two effects.

Performing a One-Sample *t* Test

1. Click *Analyze → Compare Means → One-Sample T Test*. You will see the *Paired-Samples T Test* dialog box shown in Figure 21.1.
2. Drag the variable you want to test to the *Test Variable(s)* box.
3. Enter the value in the *Test Value* box. In our example, the value is the middle CCAS score of 50.
4. Click the *OK* button and in the *Output* window you will see the results as shown in Figure 21.2.

Important Output and What It Means

- The mean score on the CCAS is 62.30, which is 12.300 (labeled mean difference) above the test value of 50. The standard deviation of the CCAS scores is 12.012.

- We are able to reject the null hypothesis that population mean is equal to 50. We reject the null hypothesis because the significance value or *p*-value (displayed as .000) is less than the traditional alpha of .05. The *p*-value is associated with the *t* value of 5.609 with degrees of freedom of 29.

- The 95 percent confidence interval of the difference between the mean CCAS and the test value ranges from 7.81 to 16.79.

- An effect size statistic—the standardized mean difference—can be computed by dividing the mean difference by the standard deviation. For our example, it is equal to 1.02; that is, 12.300 / 12.012 = 1.02, a moderate value.

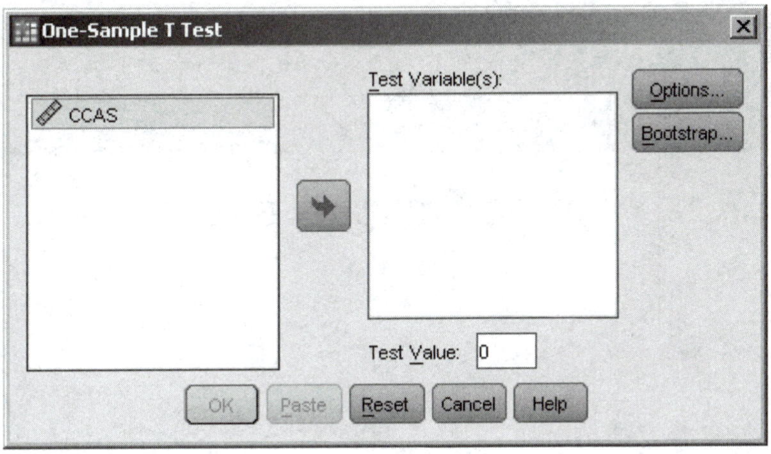

Figure 21.1 *One-Sample T Test* dialog box.

T-Test

One-Sample Statistics

	N	Mean	Std. Deviation	Std. Error Mean
CCAS	30	62.30	12.012	2.193

One-Sample Test

	Test Value = 50					
					95% Confidence Interval of the Difference	
	t	df	Sig. (2-tailed)	Mean Difference	Lower	Upper
CCAS	5.609	29	.000	12.300	7.81	16.79

Figure 21.2 Results of the One-Sample T Test.

Paired-Samples *t* Test

A paired-samples *t* test generally is used to evaluate whether the population mean of differences between paired scores is equal to zero. It frequently is applied to assess whether the mean of differences between two administrations of a test on a single population of individuals is equal to zero.

The Data

Our example data are in the file named Q22.sav.

Variable	Description
Pre_ASYC	Percent correct on the Achievement Scale for Young Children prior to involvement in the reading program
Post_ASYC	Percent correct on the Achievement Scale for Young Children after involvement in the reading program

In our example, a researcher is interested in determining whether students with a reading disability improve when exposed to an experimental reading program. Thirty students are assessed on the Achievement Scale for Young Children (ASYC) prior to and after the experimental reading program.

Performing a Paired-Sample *t* Test

To compute the test, follow these steps:

1. Click *Analyze → Compare Means → Paired-Samples T Test* and you will see the dialog box shown in Figure 22.1.
2. Click on the first variable in the pair and click ![icon] to move it to the *Variable1* location in the *Paired Variables* box. Alternatively, you can drag the variable name to the *Variable1* location.
3. Click on the second variable in the pair and click ![icon] to move it to the *Variable2* location in the *Paired Variables* box. Alternatively, you can drag the second variable to the *Variable2* location. The resulting dialog box is shown in Figure 22.2.

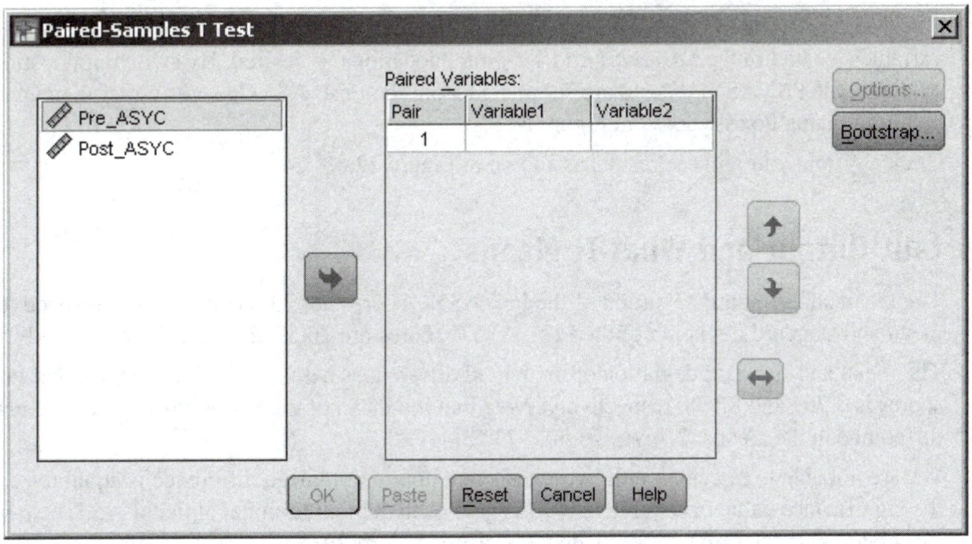

Figure 22.1 *Paired-Samples T Test* dialog box.

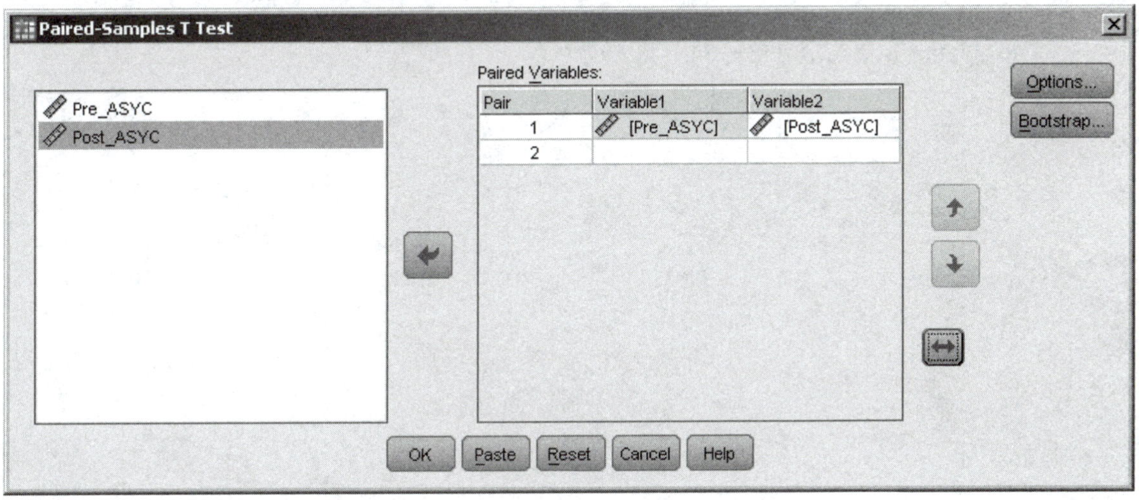

Figure 22.2 *Paired Variables* in the *Paired-Samples T Test* dialog box.

4. Click on the variable in the *Variable1* location and then click on the double-headed arrow to switch the variables located in the *Variable1* and *Variable2* locations, if desired. By switching locations in our example, the Pre_ASYC scores are subtracted from the Post_ASYC scores rather than vice versa. The resulting dialog box is shown in Figure 22.3.

5. Click *OK*, and you will see results as shown in Figure 22.4.

Important Output and What It Means

- The mean and standard deviation of the Pre_ASYC scores are 73.73 and 16.101, respectively. The mean and standard deviation of the Post_ASYC scores are 76.50 and 13.117, respectively.

- The mean and standard deviation of the paired differences between the Post_ASYC and Pre_ASYC scores is 2.767 and 8.178, respectively. Note that the mean of the paired differences is equal to the difference in the means: 2.767 = 76.50 – 73.73.

- We are not able to reject the null hypothesis that population mean difference is equal to zero because the significance value or *p*-value of .074 is greater than the traditional alpha of .05. The *p*-value is associated with the *t* of 1.853 with degrees of freedom of 29.

- The 95 percent confidence interval of the mean of the paired differences in ASYC scores ranges from –.287 to 5.820.

- An effect size statistic—the standardized mean difference—can be computed by dividing the mean of the paired differences by the standard deviation of the paired differences. For our example, it is equal to .34; that is, 2.767/8.178 = .34.

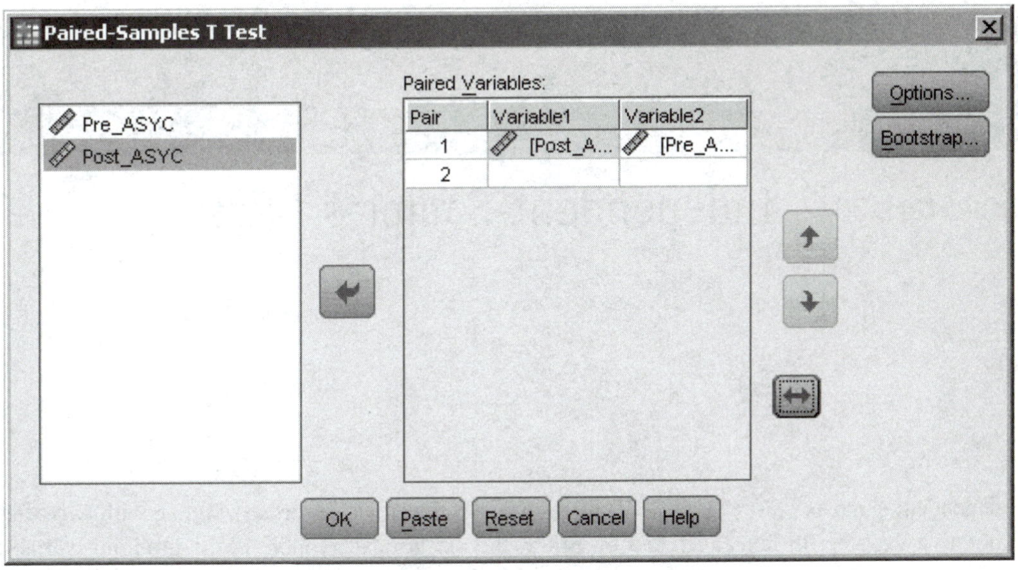

Figure 22.3 Changes to Paired Variables in the *Paired-Samples T Test* dialog box.

T-Test

Paired Samples Statistics

		Mean	N	Std. Deviation	Std. Error Mean
Pair 1	Post_ASYC	76.50	30	13.117	2.395
	Pre_ASYC	73.73	30	16.101	2.940

Paired Samples Correlations

		N	Correlation	Sig.
Pair 1	Post_ASYC & Pre_ASYC	30	.863	.000

Paired Samples Test

		Paired Differences					t	df	Sig. (2-tailed)
					95% Confidence Interval of the Difference				
		Mean	Std. Deviation	Std. Error Mean	Lower	Upper			
Pair 1	Post_ASYC - Pre_ASYC	2.767	8.178	1.493	-.287	5.820	1.853	29	.074

Figure 22.4 Results of the paired-samples *t* test.

An independent-samples *t* test examines the relationship between a categorical variable with two categories and a quantitative variable. In language used by SPSS, the categorical variable is the grouping variable, and the quantitative variable is the test variable. An independent-samples *t* test addresses the hypothesis that the population means on the dependent variable are equal across groups of the categorical variable.

The Data

Our example data are in the file named Q23.sav.

Variable	Description
Income	1 = Low; 2 = Middle
MAS	Medical Anxiety Scale

In our example, a researcher is interested in assessing whether adults who have low incomes have greater medical anxiety than adults who have moderate incomes. The researcher collects data on 11 adults with low incomes and 19 adults with middle incomes to assess her hypothesis.

Conducting an Independent-Samples *t* Test

1. Click *Analyze → Compare Means → Independent-Samples T Test*. You will see the *Independent-Samples T Test* dialog box, as shown in Figure 23.1.
2. Click the quantitative variable (e.g., MAS), and then click ▣ to move it to the *Test Variable(s)* box.
3. Click the categorical variable (e.g., Income), and then click ▣ to move it to the *Grouping Variable* box.
4. With the *Grouping Variable* box highlighted, click the *Define Groups* button and you will see the *Define Groups* dialog box. Fill in the numerical values associated with each of the two groups (1 and 2 in our example), as shown in Figure 23.2.

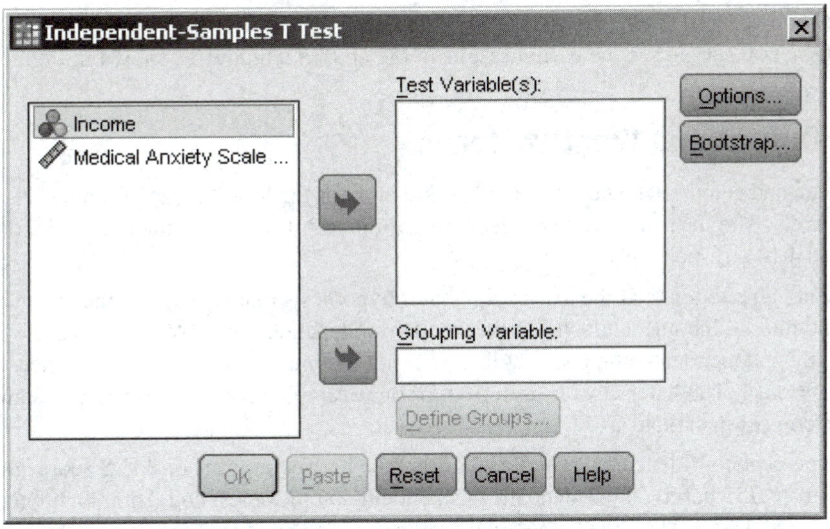

Figure 23.1 *Independent-Samples T Test* dialog box.

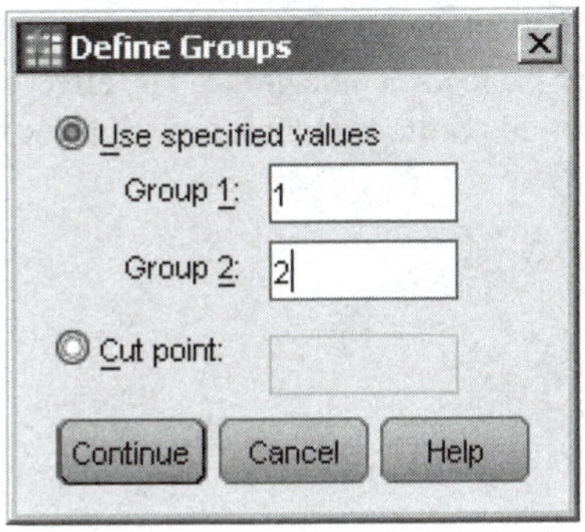

Figure 23.2 Completed *Define Groups* dialog box.

5. Click *Continue*.
6. Click *OK*. You should see the partial results in the *Output* window, as shown in Figure 23.3.

Important Output and What It Means

- The mean and standard deviation of the MAS scores for the low-income group are 15.45 and 20.825, respectively. The mean and standard deviation of the MAS scores for the middle-income group are 7.79 and 4.104, respectively.

- We are not able to reject at the .05 level the null hypothesis that population means on MAS differ for low- and middle-income adults using the standard independent-samples t test, $t(28) = 1.572$, $p = .127$, or with the independent-samples t test that does not assume homogeneity of variance, $t(10.452) = 1.207$, $p = .254$. The latter t test is preferred for our example given the disparity in standard deviations and differences in sample sizes.

- The 95 percent confidence interval of the difference between means on MAS scores ranges from –2.325 to 17.755 based on the standard independent-samples t test and from –6.399 to 21.729 based on the t test that does not assume homogeneity of variance. The latter confidence interval is preferred for our example because of reasons specified in the previous bullet point.

- An effect size statistic—the standardized mean difference—can be computed by dividing the difference in means by a standard deviation. The standard deviation may be based on one of the groups or, if they are homogeneous, pooled across groups (not computed by SPSS). For our example, we chose the standard deviation for the low-income group. The effect size was .37; that is, 7.665 / 20.825 = .37. We could have computed it based on the standard deviation for the high-income group and yielded a much different value (i.e., 1.87).

Group Statistics

	Income	N	Mean	Std. Deviation	Std. Error Mean
Medical Anxiety Scale	Low Income	11	15.45	20.825	6.279
	Middle Income	19	7.79	4.104	.942

Independent Samples Test

		Levene's Test for Equality of Variances		t-test for Equality of Means							
										95% Confidence Interval of the Difference	
		F	Sig.	t	df	Sig. (2-tailed)	Mean Difference	Std. Error Difference	Lower	Upper
Medical Anxiety Scale	Equal variances assumed	4.337	.047	1.572	28	.127	7.665	4.877	-2.325	17.655
	Equal variances not assumed			1.207	10.452	.254	7.665	6.349	-6.399	21.729

Figure 23.3   Results of the independent samples *t* test.

One-Way Analysis of Variance

A one-way analysis of variance (one-way ANOVA) examines the relationship between a categorical variable and a quantitative variable. In language used by SPSS, the categorical variable is the factor, and the quantitative variable is the dependent variable. A one-way ANOVA addresses the hypothesis that the population means on the dependent variables are the same for all levels (i.e., categories) of the factor.

The Data

Our example data are in the file named Q24.sav.

Variable	Description
Intervention	1 = no treatment; 2 = Systematic Desensitization; 3 = Hypnosis
FOST	Fear of Spider Test

In our example, a researcher is interested in determining which treatment approach is best for adults with spider phobias: none, systematic desensitization, or hypnosis. Sixty adults with spider phobias are randomly assigned to the three treatment approaches. After a month of treatment (or no treatment), they are assessed on the FOST.

Conducting a One-Way Analysis of Variance

1. *Click Analyze → Compare Means → One-Way ANOVA.* You will see the *One-Way ANOVA* dialog box as shown in Figure 24.1.
2. Click the quantitative variable (e.g., FOST), and then click ⮇ to move it to the *Dependent List* box.
3. Click the categorical variable (e.g., Intervention), and then click ⮇ to move it to the *Factor* box.
4. Click *Options*, and you will see the *One-Way ANOVA: Options* dialog box, as shown in Figure 24.2. Choose *Descriptive, Homogeneity of variance test*, and *Welch* in the *Statistics* box. Click *Continue*.

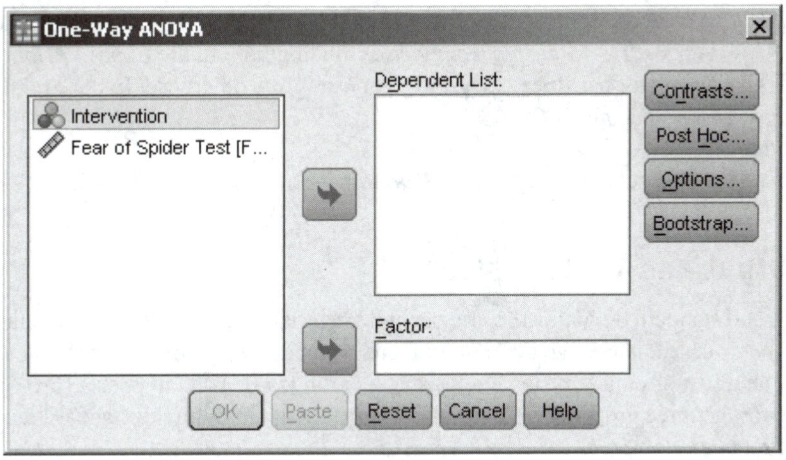

Figure 24.1 *One-Way ANOVA* dialog box.

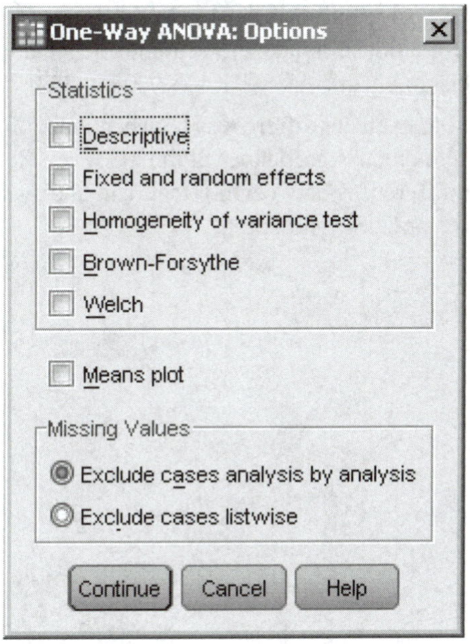

Figure 24.2 *One-Way ANOVA: Options* dialog box.

5. Click *Post Hoc* to evaluate comparisons between pairs of levels of the factor. You should see the *One-Way ANOVA: Post Hoc Multiple Comparisons* dialog box. In the *Equal Variances Assumed* box, choose *LSD* if your factor has three categories; choose *Tukey* otherwise. In the *Equal Variances Not Assumed* box, choose *Dunnett's C*.
6. Click *Continue*.
7. Click *OK*. You should see the results in the *Output* window, as shown in Figures 24.3 and 24.4.

Important Output and What It Means

- The means and standard deviations on the dependent variable for each level of the factor are typically reported. In this case, on average the no-treatment group did worse on the fear scale (73.70) than either of the two treatment groups—systematic desensitization (54.75) and hypnosis (69.05). The standard deviations for the three groups were not radically different, although the standard deviation for the hypnosis group was lower.

- The ANOVA was significant at the .05 level, $F(2, 57) = 6.877$, $p = .002$, so the hypothesis that the population means on FOST scores are equal for the three treatments can be rejected. The Welch method evaluates the same hypothesis, but does not require the homogeneity-of-variance assumption. The hypothesis was also rejected with this test, $F(2, 37.430) = 5.866$, $p = .006$.

- We computed a strength-of-relationship index, the sample eta square, by dividing the between-group sum of squares by the total sum of squares: 3901.433 / 20070.333 = .19.

- Comparisons were assessed to evaluate differences between pairs of population means. Stars (*) in the Multiple Comparisons table indicate significance at the .05 level. Regardless of choice of statistical test, there were significant differences between no treatment and systematic desensitization and between hypnosis and systematic desensitization.

Oneway

Descriptives

Fear of Spider Test

	N	Mean	Std. Deviation	Std. Error	95% Confidence Interval for Mean		Minimum	Maximum
					Lower Bound	Upper Bound		
None	20	73.70	17.284	3.865	65.61	81.79	38	99
Systematic Desensitization	20	54.75	18.764	4.196	45.97	63.53	29	91
Hypnosis	20	69.05	14.148	3.164	62.43	75.67	42	91
Total	60	65.83	18.444	2.381	61.07	70.60	29	99

ANOVA

Fear of Spider Test

	Sum of Squares	df	Mean Square	F	Sig.
Between Groups	3901.433	2	1950.717	6.877	.002
Within Groups	16168.900	57	283.665		
Total	20070.333	59			

Figure 24.3 Partial results of One-Way ANOVA.

Post Hoc Tests

Multiple Comparisons

Dependent Variable:Fear of Spider Test

	(I) Intervention	(J) Intervention	Mean Difference (I-J)	Std. Error	Sig.	95% Confidence Interval	
						Lower Bound	Upper Bound
LSD	None	Systematic Desensitization	18.950[*]	5.326	.001	8.28	29.62
		Hypnosis	4.650	5.326	.386	-6.02	15.32
	Systematic Desensitization	None	-18.950[*]	5.326	.001	-29.62	-8.28
		Hypnosis	-14.300[*]	5.326	.009	-24.97	-3.63
	Hypnosis	None	-4.650	5.326	.386	-15.32	6.02
		Systematic Desensitization	14.300[*]	5.326	.009	3.63	24.97
Dunnett C	None	Systematic Desensitization	18.950[*]	5.705		4.46	33.44
		Hypnosis	4.650	4.995		-8.04	17.34
	Systematic Desensitization	None	-18.950[*]	5.705		-33.44	-4.46
		Hypnosis	-14.300[*]	5.255		-27.65	-.95
	Hypnosis	None	-4.650	4.995		-17.34	8.04
		Systematic Desensitization	14.300[*]	5.255		.95	27.65

*.The mean difference is significant at the 0.05 level.

Figure 24.4 Partial results of One-Way ANOVA (continued).

One-Way Repeated-Measures Analysis of Variance

A one-way repeated-measures analysis of variance (ANOVA) examines the relationship between a repeated-measures categorical variable and a quantitative dependent variable. The repeated-measures variable is also called a within-subjects factor. The scores on the quantitative variable are dependent across levels of the within-subjects factor, typically because each individual provides scores for all levels of the factor. A separate variable is defined in the SPSS data file for the scores on the dependent variable for each level of the factor, and the factor is defined in the dialog boxes when conducting the analysis. This test evaluates the hypothesis that the population means on the dependent variable are equal across all levels of the factor.

The Data

Our example data is in the file named Q25.sav.

Variable	Description
Math	Effectiveness ratings of their high school math teachers
English	Effectiveness ratings of their high school English teachers
History	Effectiveness ratings of their high school history teachers

A researcher is interested in assessing whether high school graduates evaluate differentially the instructional effectiveness of their teachers in math, English, and history. She asks 25 recent high school graduates to rate the instructional effectiveness of their math, English, and history teachers. The factor is the subject matter taught, and the dependent variable is instructional effectiveness.

Conducting a One-Way Repeated-Measures ANOVA

1. Click *Analyze → General Linear Model → Repeated Measures*, and you will see the *Repeated Measures Define Factor(s)* dialog box as shown in Figure 25.1.

2. In the *Within-Subject Factor Name* box, type a name for your within-subjects factor (e.g., Subject_Taught).

3. Enter the number of levels of the within-subjects factor in the *Number of Levels* box (e.g., 3), and click *Add*.

4. Click *Define*, and you will see the *Repeated Measures* dialog box as shown in Figure 25.2.

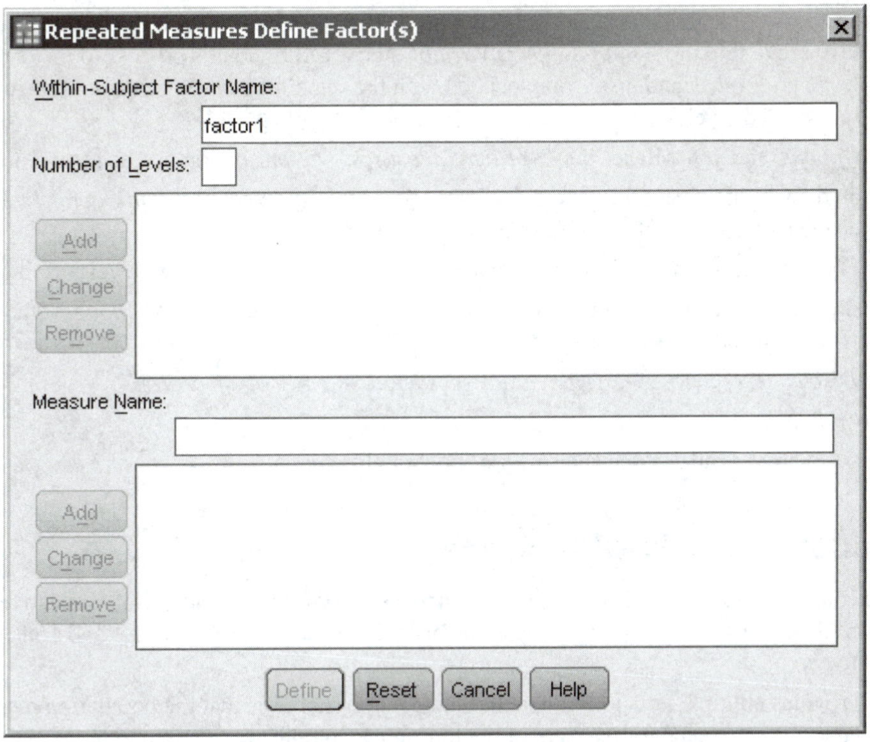

Figure 25.1 *Repeated Measures Define Factor(s)* dialog box.

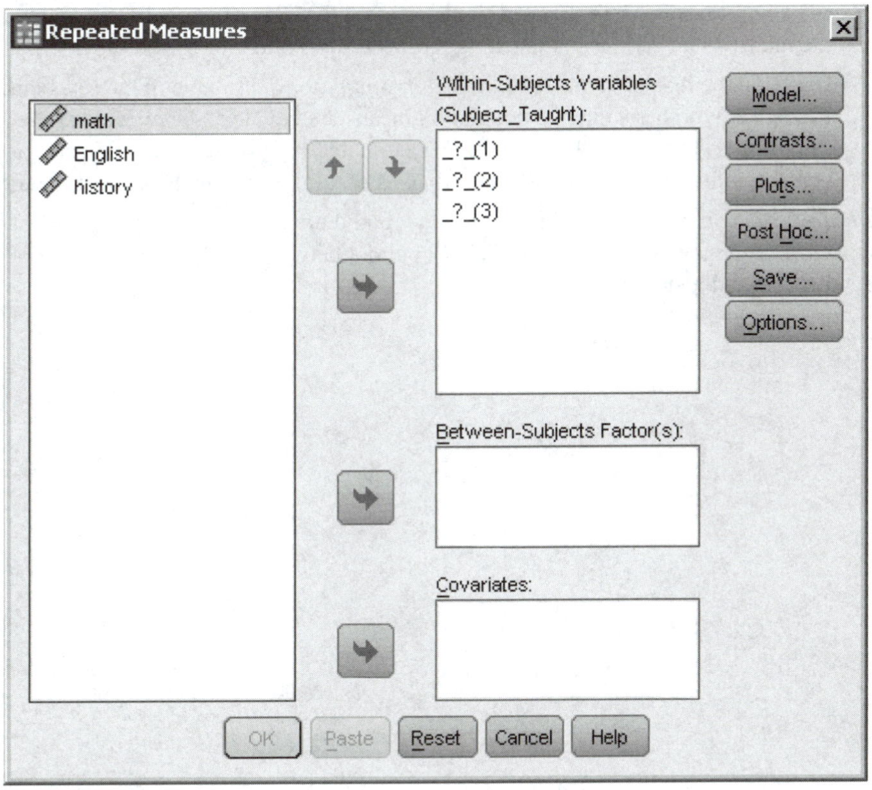

Figure 25.2 *Repeated Measures* dialog box.

5. Click on the variable (e.g., *math*) associated with the first level of the within-subjects factor, and then click ⊡ to move it to the *Within-Subjects Variables* box. Continue this process to move the other variables (e.g., *English* and *history*) associated with the remaining levels of the within-subjects factor (e.g., 2nd and 3rd levels).

6. Click *Options*, and you will see the *Repeated Measures: Options* dialog box as shown in Figure 25.3.

7. Click on the within-subject factor (e.g., *Subject_Taught*) in the *Factor(s) and Factor Interactions* box, and then click ⊡ to move it to the *Display Means for* box.

8. Click *Compare main effects* if the within-subjects factor has more than two levels, as in our example.

9. In the drop down menu labeled *Confidence interval adjustment*, choose *LSD(none)* if the within-subjects factor has three levels; otherwise, choose *Sidak*.

10. In the *Display* box, choose *Descriptive statistics* and *Estimates of effect size*.

11. Click *Continue*.

12. Click *OK*. Partial results of the analysis are shown in Figure 25.4.

Important Output and What It Means

- The means for math, English, and history teachers are 50.04, 58.16, and 53.62, respectively. The standard deviations for math, English, and history teachers are 16.797, 20.655, and 16.536, respectively.

- SPSS provides multiple tests to evaluate the same null hypothesis that the population means of teaching ratings are equal for teachers of math, English, and history. Only one of these tests needs to be presented in a research paper. We focus on two of these tests.

    o The results in the *Wilks' lambda* row of the *Multivariate Tests* table indicate the hypothesis that the population means are equal can be rejected at the .05 level, Wilks' $\Lambda = .769$, $F(2, 23) = 3.464$, $p = .048$. The estimated multivariate η^2 is .231, which indicates about 23 percent of the multivariate variance of teaching ratings is accounted for by the subject matter taught.

    o Based on the results in the *Tests of Within-Subjects Effects* table in the rows labeled *Huynh-Feldt*, the hypothesis that the population means are equal can be rejected at the .05 level, $F(1.745, 41.880) = 3.934$, $p = .032$. The estimated η^2 is .141, which indicates about 14 percent of the variance of teaching ratings is accounted for by the subject matter taught.

- In the *Pairwise Comparison* table, the results show that there is a statistically significant mean difference between math and English ($p = .019$), but not between math and history ($p = .104$) or between English and history ($p = .173$).

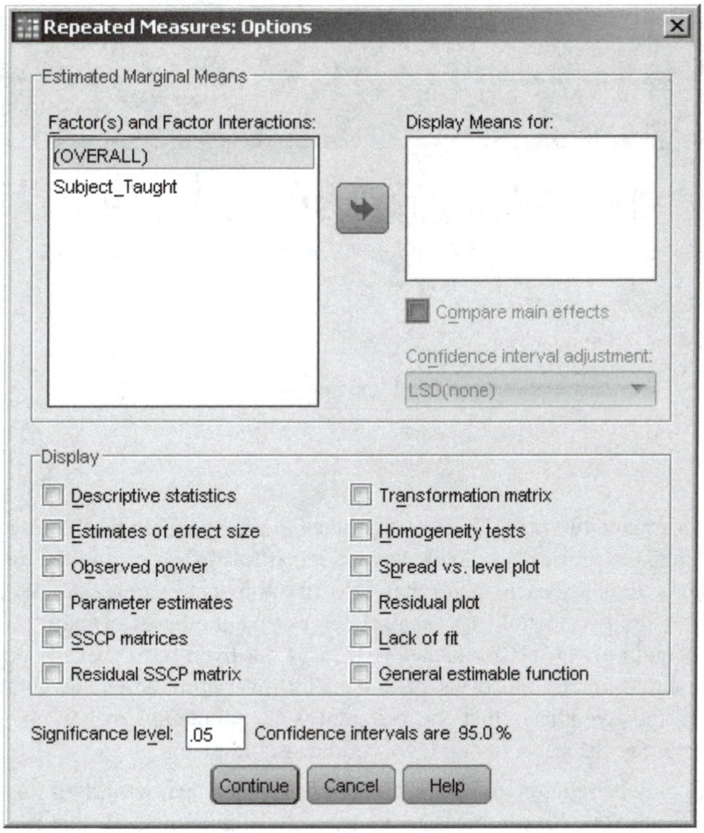

Figure 25.3 *Repeated Measures: Options* dialog box.

Multivariate Tests[b]

Effect		Value	F	Hypothesis df	Error df	Sig.	Partial Eta Squared
Subject_Taught	Pillai's Trace	.231	3.464[a]	2.000	23.000	.048	.231
	Wilks' Lambda	.769	3.464[a]	2.000	23.000	.048	.231
	Hotelling's Trace	.301	3.464[a]	2.000	23.000	.048	.231
	Roy's Largest Root	.301	3.464[a]	2.000	23.000	.048	.231

a. Exact statistic

b. Design: Intercept
Within Subjects Design: Subject_Taught

Tests of Within-Subjects Effects

Measure:MEASURE_1

Source		Type III Sum of Squares	df	Mean Square	F	Sig.	Partial Eta Squared
Subject_Taught	Sphericity Assumed	828.020	2	414.010	3.934	.026	.141
	Greenhouse-Geisser	828.020	1.641	504.681	3.934	.035	.141
	Huynh-Feldt	828.020	1.745	474.510	3.934	.032	.141
	Lower-bound	828.020	1.000	828.020	3.934	.059	.141
Error(Subject_Taught)	Sphericity Assumed	5051.813	48	105.246			
	Greenhouse-Geisser	5051.813	39.376	128.296			
	Huynh-Feldt	5051.813	41.880	120.626			
	Lower-bound	5051.813	24.000	210.492			

Figure 25.4 Partial results of the one-way repeated-measures analysis of variance.

Two-Way Analysis of Variance

A two-way analysis of variance (2-way ANOVA) examines the relationship between two categorical variables and a quantitative variable. Categorical variables may be called fixed factors, and the quantitative variable may be called the dependent variable. Each factor has two or more categories (i.e., levels), and cells are the combinations of levels of the two factors. The analysis assesses hypotheses of main effects of the two factors and their interaction. A main effect test for a factor assesses the hypothesis that the population means on the dependent variable are equal among all levels of that factor, averaging across levels of the other factor. An interaction test assesses the hypothesis that the differences in population means on the dependent variable among levels of one factor are the same among levels of the second factor.

Complex methods may be required to conduct a 2-way ANOVA, particularly if the number of respondents differs among cells. In QuickStart 26, we illustrate procedurally simple methods that can be done through SPSS dialog boxes. We first show how to test the main and interaction effects. We then demonstrate how to conduct tests to further explore main effects if a factor has more than two levels and interaction effects are minimal. Finally we demonstrate how to perform simple main effect tests in the presence of interaction effects. The decisions required in conducting a two-way ANOVA involve judgments about your data in the context of your research questions and the design of your study. An ANOVA textbook should be consulted to help you make these decisions. You also may need to consult our more detailed book on SPSS to conduct alternative two-way ANOVA methods.

The Data

Our example data are in the file named Q26.sav.

Variable	Description
Intensity	1 = High, 2 = Moderate, 3 = Low
Amount	1 = Twice a week, 2 = Daily
Change_Speed	Time prior to training – time after training

In our example, a researcher is interested in determining what type of weight training program will produce the most improved times in swimming a 1000-meter freestyle event for 1st year high school boys who are intermediate-level swimmers. She randomly assigns 360 freshmen to weight training either daily or two days per week, with the restriction that the numbers of students are equal across groups. Within each of the two groups, she randomly assigns 60 students each to low, medium, and high intensity workouts. The dependent variable is computed by subtracting the finishing time in the event after completing weight training for 3 months from the finishing time in the event before training.

Conducting a Two-Way Analysis of Variance

1. Click *Analyze* → *General Linear Model* → *Univariate,* and you will see the dialog box shown in Figure 26.1.

2. Click the name of the dependent variable (e.g., Change_Speed), and then click ⬇ to move it to the *Dependent Variable* box.

3. Click on the name of one of the factors (e.g., Intensity), and then click ⬇ to move it to the *Fixed Factor(s)* box.

4. Click on the name of other factor (e.g., Amount), and then click ⬇ to move it to the *Fixed Factor(s)* box.

5. Click the *Options* button as shown in Figure 26.2.

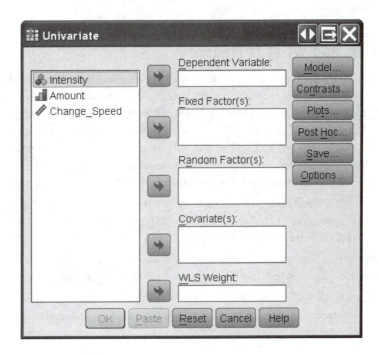

Figure 26.1 *Univariate* dialog box.

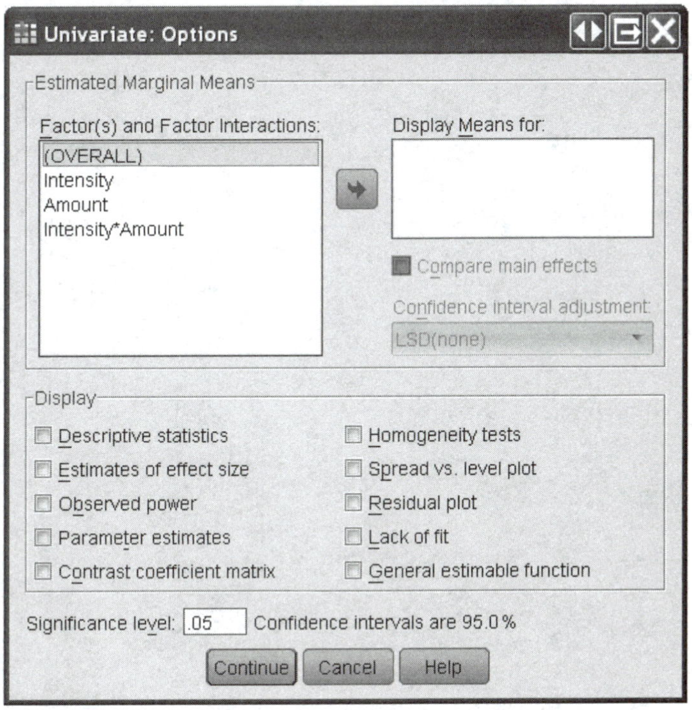

Figure 26.2 *Univariate: Options* dialog box.

6. In the *Univariate: Options* dialog box, double click on the names of the factors (e.g., Intensity and Amount) and their interaction (e.g., Intensity*Amount) in the *Factor(s) and Factor Interaction* box to move them to the *Display Means for* box.

7. In the same dialog box, click *Descriptive statistics*, *Estimates of effect sizes*, and *Homogeneity tests* in the *Display* area.

8. Click *Continue*.

9. Click *OK*, and you will see the two-way ANOVA results. Partial results for the example are shown in Figures 26.3 and 26.4.

Important Output and What It Means

- The *Descriptive Statistics* and *Estimated Marginal Means* tables show the means for the main effects as well as the cell means. For example, for the main effect of amount of training, freshmen who weight trained daily improved on average 14.352 seconds, while those who weight trained twice a week improved on average 12.083 seconds. The two types of tables generally yield comparable results for cell means, but potentially generate different means for the main effects if sample sizes are unequal across cells. Note that the *Descriptive Statistics* table includes standard deviations, whereas the *Estimated Marginal Means* table contains standard errors and confidence intervals.

- The main effect for Intensity was significant at the .05 level, $F(2, 354) = 13.490$, $p < .001$, as well as the main effect for Amount, $F(1, 354) = 31.723$, $p < .001$. In addition, the interaction between Intensity and Amount was significant at the .05 level, $F(2, 354) = 3.187$, p = .042.

- The partial eta squares, a strength of relationship index, were moderate in size for the main effects (i.e., .071 and .082 for Intensity and Amount, respectively) and small in size for the interaction (i.e., .018).

- Typically follow-up tests of main effects are conducted only if interaction effects are weak. In the presence of an interaction, simple main effect tests are generally conducted. For our example data, an argument could be made for both types of follow-up tests. We demonstrate both types of follow-up tests next.

Dependent Variable:Change_Speed

Intensity	Amount	Mean	Std. Deviation	N
Low	Twice a week	11.520	3.6967	60
	Daily	13.103	3.3375	60
	Total	12.312	3.5958	120
Medium	Twice a week	11.898	4.5346	60
	Daily	13.415	4.1768	60
	Total	12.657	4.4073	120
High	Twice a week	12.830	3.5746	60
	Daily	16.537	3.4696	60
	Total	14.683	3.9708	120
Total	Twice a week	12.083	3.9747	180
	Daily	14.352	3.9757	180
	Total	13.217	4.1290	360

Estimated Marginal Means

1. Intensity

Dependent Variable:Change_Speed

Intensity			95% Confidence Interval	
	Mean	Std. Error	Lower Bound	Upper Bound
Low	12.312	.349	11.626	12.998
Medium	12.657	.349	11.971	13.343
High	14.683	.349	13.997	15.369

2. Amount

Dependent Variable:Change_Speed

Amount			95% Confidence Interval	
	Mean	Std. Error	Lower Bound	Upper Bound
Twice a week	12.083	.285	11.523	12.643
Daily	14.352	.285	13.791	14.912

Figure 26.3   Partial results of the two-way analysis of variance.

Tests of Between-Subjects Effects

Dependent Variable:Change_Speed

Source	Type III Sum of Squares	df	Mean Square	F	Sig.	Partial Eta Squared
Corrected Model	950.446[a]	5	190.089	13.015	.000	.155
Intercept	62890.187	1	62890.187	4306.108	.000	.924
Intensity	394.048	2	197.024	13.490	.000	.071
Amount	463.307	1	463.307	31.723	.000	.082
Intensity * Amount	93.091	2	46.545	3.187	.042	.018
Error	5170.127	354	14.605			
Total	69010.760	360				
Corrected Total	6120.573	359				

a. R Squared = .155 (Adjusted R Squared = .143)

Figure 26.4   Partial results of the two-way analysis of variance (continued).

Conducting Follow-Up Tests to Main Effects

If the main effect for a factor with more than two levels is significant and the interaction effect is minimal, tests may be conducted to assess pairwise differences in means among levels of that factor. The *Post Hoc* dialog box can be used to conduct pairwise comparisons. However, we do not use this approach in that the results based on it are not follow-up tests to the main effects, as we conducted them, if sample sizes differ among cells. For our example, we show how to conduct tests to assess pairwise mean differences among the three levels of the Intensity factor.

1. Click *Analyze → General Linear Model → Univariate*.

2. Click the *Reset* button.

3. Conduct steps 2 through 4 as described previously.

4. Click the *Options* button.

5. In the *Univariate: Options* dialog box, double click on the name of the factor associated with the follow-up tests (e.g., Intensity) in the *Factor(s) and Factor Interaction* box and move it to the *Display Means for* box.

6. Click in the box next to *Compare main effects* in the same dialog box.

7. In the drop down menu labeled *Confidence interval adjustment*, choose one of the options. If the factor of interest (e.g., Intensity) has three levels, we recommend choosing *LSD (none)*; otherwise, choose one of the other two options. The completed *Univariate: Options* for this example is shown in Figure 26.5.

8. Click *Continue*.

9. Click *OK*, and you will see the results for the pairwise comparisons for Intensity, as shown in Figure 26.6.

Important Output and What It Means

- The *Pairwise Comparisons* table gives the follow-up tests for Intensity. The mean difference between low and medium intensity of -.345 is nonsignificant, $p = .485$.

- The mean difference between low and high intensity of -2.372 and the mean difference between medium and high intensity of -2.027 were significant, both with p-values of less than .001.

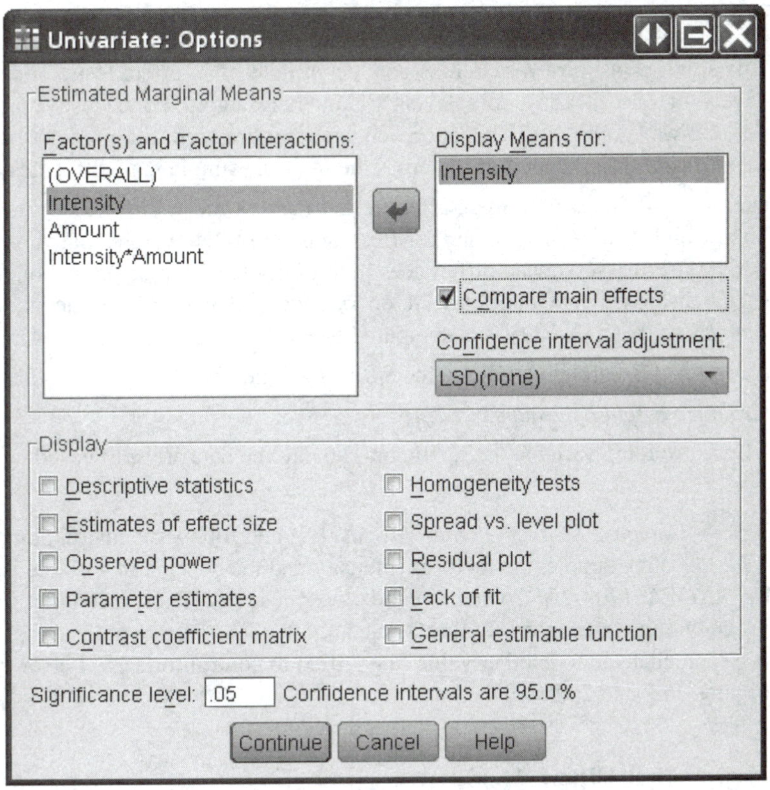

Figure 26.5 *Univariate: Options box for* follow-up tests to main effects.

Pairwise Comparisons

Dependent Variable:Change_Speed

(I) Intensity	(J) Intensity	Mean Difference (I-J)	Std. Error	Sig.[a]	95% Confidence Interval for Difference[a]	
					Lower Bound	Upper Bound
Low	Medium	-.345	.493	.485	-1.315	.625
	High	-2.372[*]	.493	.000	-3.342	-1.401
Medium	Low	.345	.493	.485	-.625	1.315
	High	-2.027[*]	.493	.000	-2.997	-1.056
High	Low	2.372[*]	.493	.000	1.401	3.342
	Medium	2.027[*]	.493	.000	1.056	2.997

Based on estimated marginal means

a. Adjustment for multiple comparisons: Least Significant Difference (equivalent to no adjustments).

*. The mean difference is significant at the .05 level.

Figure 26.6 Results of follow-up tests to main effects.

Conducting Follow-Up Tests to Interaction Effects

If an interaction test is significant, most researchers conduct simple main effect tests. These tests assess mean difference among levels of one factor within levels of another factor. These tests may be performed by conducting a series of one-way ANOVAs. This approach is straightforward, but may not be the most powerful method. You may want to control for Type I error across the multiple simple main effect tests.

For our example, we examine simple main effect tests to assess mean differences among intensity levels for freshmen who lifted weights twice a week and for freshmen who lifted weights daily. More specifically, we compute a one-way ANOVA to assess mean differences in intensity level for each level of Amount. These tests use methods previously discussed in QuickStart 24 on one-way ANOVA. The file is split using methods described in QuickStart 13 so that an ANOVA is computed for each of the two levels of Amount.

1. Click *Data → Split File*, and you will see the *Split File* dialog box.
2. Click the *Organize output by groups* button.
3. Double click the grouping variable (e.g., Amount) so that the data are split based on this variable.
4. Click *OK*.
5. Click *Analyze → Compare Means → One-Way ANOVA* and follow the instruction described in QuickStart 24. For our example, the factor is Intensity and the dependent variable is Change_Speed. In the *One-Way ANOVA: Post Hoc Comparison* box, we chose *LSD* tests to conduct pairwise comparisons among the three intensity levels. We kept the *Significance level* at the .05 level, although it might have been changed to another value (e.g., .025) to control for Type I error rate. The results are shown in Figures 26.7 and 26.8.

Important Output and What It Means

- The one-way ANOVA was nonsignificant for freshmen who weight trained twice a week, $F(2, 177) = 1.741$, $p = .178$.

- The one-way ANOVA was significant for freshmen who weight trained daily, $F(2, 177) = 15.973$, $p < .001$.

- Pairwise comparisons are presented in the Multiple Comparisons tables among levels of Intensity within each level of Amount. However, the results for freshmen who weight trained twice a week were ignored because the one-way ANOVA for these students was nonsignificant.

- For freshmen who weight trained daily, the difference in means between low and medium intensity training of −.3117 is nonsignificant, $p = .643$. The other two pairwise comparisons were significant: mean difference of −3.4333 and $p < .001$ for the low versus high intensity comparison and mean difference of −3.1217 and $p < .001$ for the medium versus high intensity comparison.

Amount = Twice a week

ANOVA[a]

Change_Speed

	Sum of Squares	df	Mean Square	F	Sig.
Between Groups	54.545	2	27.272	1.741	.178
Within Groups	2773.352	177	15.669		
Total	2827.897	179			

a. Amount = Twice a week

Post Hoc Tests

Multiple Comparisons[a]

Change_Speed
LSD

(I) Intensity	(J) Intensity	Mean Difference (I-J)	Std. Error	Sig.	95% Confidence Interval	
					Lower Bound	Upper Bound
Low	Medium	-.3783	.7227	.601	-1.805	1.048
	High	-1.3100	.7227	.072	-2.736	.116
Medium	Low	.3783	.7227	.601	-1.048	1.805
	High	-.9317	.7227	.199	-2.358	.495
High	Low	1.3100	.7227	.072	-.116	2.736
	Medium	.9317	.7227	.199	-.495	2.358

a. Amount = Twice a week

Figure 26.7 Results of simple main effect tests for freshmen who trained twice a week.

Amount = Daily

ANOVA[a]

Change_Speed

	Sum of Squares	df	Mean Square	F	Sig.
Between Groups	432.594	2	216.297	15.973	.000
Within Groups	2396.775	177	13.541		
Total	2829.370	179			

a. Amount = Daily

Post Hoc Tests

Multiple Comparisons[a]

Change_Speed
LSD

(I) Intensity	(J) Intensity	Mean Difference (I-J)	Std. Error	Sig.	95% Confidence Interval	
					Lower Bound	Upper Bound
Low	Medium	-.3117	.6718	.643	-1.638	1.014
	High	-3.4333*	.6718	.000	-4.759	-2.107
Medium	Low	.3117	.6718	.643	-1.014	1.638
	High	-3.1217*	.6718	.000	-4.448	-1.796
High	Low	3.4333*	.6718	.000	2.107	4.759
	Medium	3.1217*	.6718	.000	1.796	4.448

*. The mean difference is significant at the 0.05 level.

a. Amount = Daily

Figure 26.8 Results of simple main effect tests for freshmen who trained daily.

PART VII

QuickStart 27 | Pearson Product-Moment Correlation Coefficient

The Pearson product-moment correlation is a numerical index that reflects the strength of linear relationship between two quantitative variables. It ranges from −1 (i.e., perfect inverse relationship) to +1 (i.e., perfect direct relationship). The value of 0 indicates no linear relationship between variables. A t test evaluates the null hypothesis that the population Pearson product-moment correlation is equal to 0. A scatterplot is created to develop a more complete understanding of the relationship between variables.

The Data

Our example data are in the file named Q27.sav.

Variable	Description
Latency	Mean response time for 30 geometric puzzles
Accuracy	Total number correct for 30 geometric puzzles

In our example, a researcher is interested in the relationship between the mean response time and the total number correct for 30 geometric puzzles. She obtains scores on 25 adults who are between the ages of 70 and 80 and are not cognitively impaired.

Computing a Pearson Product-Moment Correlation Coefficient

1. Click *Analyze* → *Correlate* → *Bivariate*, and you will see the *Bivariate Correlation* dialog box, as shown in Figure 27.1.
2. Double click on the variables (e.g., Latency and Accuracy) you want to move to the *Variables* box.
3. Ensure that default options are selected: *Pearson, Two-tailed*, and *Flag significant correlations*.
4. Click the *Options* button and you will see the *Bivariate Correlations: Options* dialog box. Click *Means and Standard Deviations*. Click *Continue*.
5. Click *OK*, and you will see the results of the analysis in Figure 27.2.

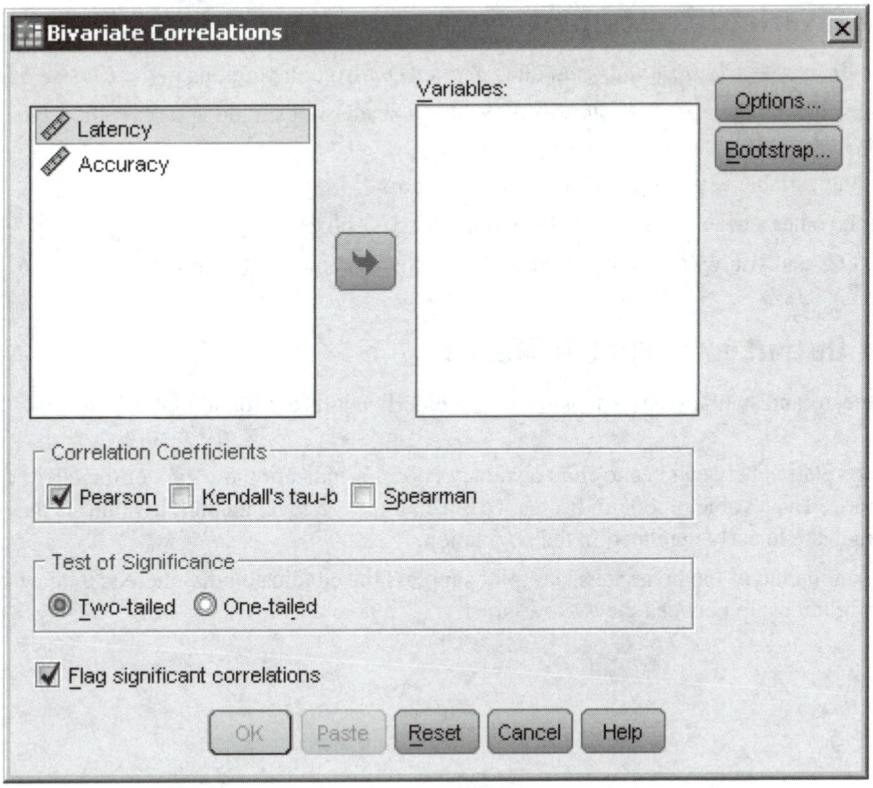

Figure 27.1 *Bivariate Correlations* dialog box.

Correlations

Descriptive Statistics

	Mean	Std. Deviation	N
Latency	25.388	12.4730	25
Accuracy	12.32	6.060	25

Correlations

		Latency	Accuracy
Latency	Pearson Correlation	1	-.545[**]
	Sig. (2-tailed)		.005
	N	25	25
Accuracy	Pearson Correlation	-.545[**]	1
	Sig. (2-tailed)	.005	
	N	25	25

Figure 27.2 Results of the bivariate correlational analysis.

Creating a Bivariate Scatterplot

1. Click *Graphs → Chart Builder*, and click *Scatter/Dot* from the options in the *Choose from* box.
2. Double click on the *Simple Scatter* icon. A simple scatterplot should appear in the *Chart Builder* dialog box, as shown in Figure 27.3.
3. Drag one variable (e.g., *Latency*) to the *Y-Axis?* box.
4. Drag the other variable (e.g., *Accuracy*) to the *X-Axis?* box.
5. Click *OK,* and you will see the bivariate scatterplot, as shown in Figure 27.4.

Important Output and What It Means

- The means and standard deviations for the 25 elderly adults are found in the *Descriptive Statistics* table.
- The correlation between latency and accuracy is $-.545$, indicating the greater the latency the less the accuracy. The *p* value of .005 indicates we reject at the .05 level the null hypothesis that latency and accuracy are linearly unrelated in the population.
- An examination of the bivariate scatterplot supports the conclusion that there is a fairly strong negative linear relationship between the two variables.

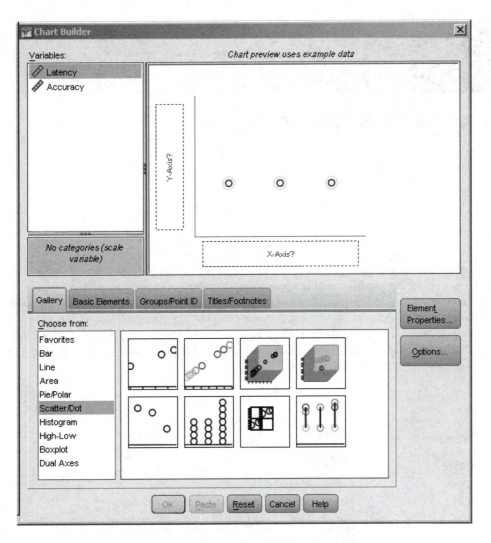

Figure 27.3 Selection of a simple scatterplot in the *Chart Builder* dialog box.

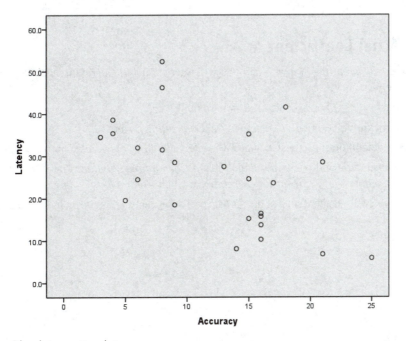

Figure 27.4 Bivariate scatterplot.

The partial correlation coefficient is an index assessing the linear relationship between two variables, statistically controlling for a third variable (or multiple variables). Another way of describing "statistically controlling for a third variable" is "partialing out the effects of a third variable." When applied appropriately, it may be interpreted as the correlation between two variables for any specific value of the control variable(s). Like a bivariate correlation, the partial correlation ranges in value from -1 to $+1$. A t test evaluates the null hypothesis that the population partial correlation is 0. A 3-D scatterplot can be created to develop a more complete understanding of partial relationships.

The Data

Our example data are in the file named Q28.sav.

Variable	Description
Interest	Interest in geometric puzzles
Latency	Mean response time for 30 geometric puzzles
Accuracy	Total number correct for 30 geometric puzzles

In our example, a researcher wishes to evaluate the relationship between interest in geometric puzzles and accuracy in solving them, holding constant latency in response time. Scores are available for 25 non-cognitively impaired women between the ages of 70 and 80.

Computing a Partial Coefficient

1. Click *Analyze* → *Correlate* → *Partial,* and you will see the *Partial Correlations* dialog box, as shown in Figure 28.1.
2. Move the variables (e.g., *Interest* and *Accuracy*) to the *Variables* box.
3. Move the control variable(s) (e.g., *Latency*) to the *Controlling for* box.
4. Ensure that the default options are selected: *Two-tailed* and *Display actual significance level.*
5. Click the *Options* button and you will see the *Partial Correlations: Options* dialog box. Click *Means and standard deviations* and *Zero-order correlations.* Click *Continue.*
6. Click *OK*, and you will see the results of the partial correlation analysis, as shown in Figure 28.2.

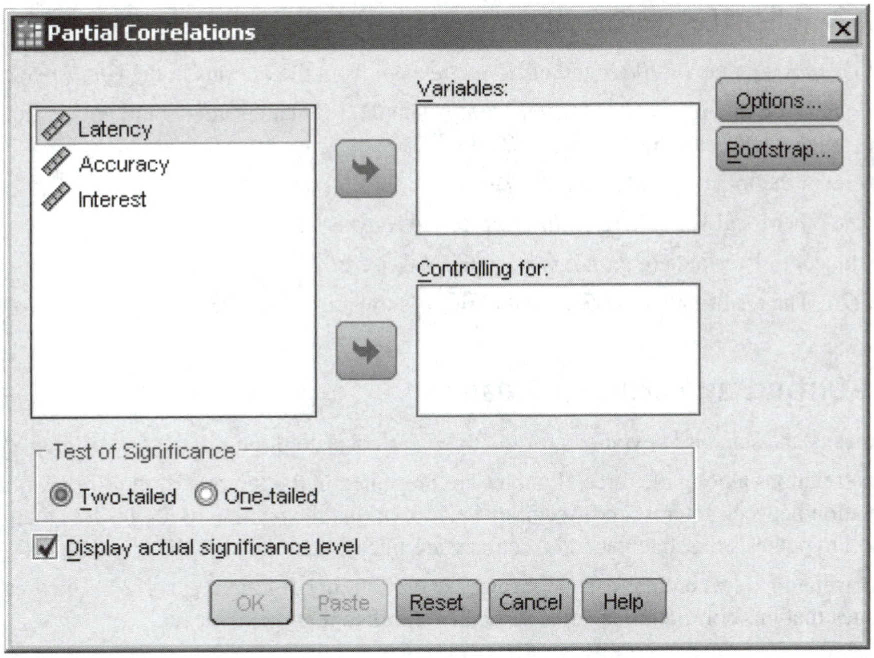

Figure 28.1 *Partial Correlations* dialog box.

Descriptive Statistics

	Mean	Std. Deviation	N
Interest	49.280	35.7917	25
Accuracy	12.320	6.0603	25
Latency	25.388	12.4730	25

Correlations

Control Variables			Interest	Accuracy	Latency
-none-[a]	Interest	Correlation	1.000	.466	-.723
		Significance (2-tailed)	.	.019	.000
		df	0	23	23
	Accuracy	Correlation	.466	1.000	-.545
		Significance (2-tailed)	.019	.	.005
		df	23	0	23
	Latency	Correlation	-.723	-.545	1.000
		Significance (2-tailed)	.000	.005	.
		df	23	23	0
Latency	Interest	Correlation	1.000	.124	
		Significance (2-tailed)	.	.563	
		df	0	22	
	Accuracy	Correlation	.124	1.000	
		Significance (2-tailed)	.563	.	
		df	22	0	

a. Cells contain zero-order (Pearson) correlations.

Figure 28.2 Results of the partial correlational analysis.

Creating a 3-D Scatterplot

1. Click *Graphs* → *Chart Builder* and click *Scatter/Dot* from the options in the *Choose from* box.
2. Double click on the *Simple 3-D Scatter* icon. A simple 3-D scatterplot should appear in the *Chart Builder* dialog box, as shown in Figure 28.3.
3. Drag one of the focal variables (e.g., *Accuracy*) to the *Y-Axis?* box.
4. Drag the other focal variable (e.g., Interest) to the X-Axis? box.
5. Drag the control variable (e.g., *Latency*) to the *Z-Axis?* box.
6. Click *OK*. The resulting simple 3-D scatterplot is shown in Figure 28.4.

Important Output and What It Means

*   The means and standard deviations for the three variables are found in the *Descriptive Statistics* table.
*   The correlations among the three variables are presented in the top part of the *Correlations* table. The correlation between Interest and Accuracy is .466. In that the *p* value of .019 is less than .05, we reject the null hypothesis that Interest and Accuracy are linearly unrelated in the population.
*   The correlation between Interest and Accuracy, partialling out Latency, is .124. The *p* value of .563 indicates that this correlation is not statistically significant at the .05 level.

A word of caution with 3-D scatterplots: They are visually impressive, but difficult to interpret. Consistent with a partial correlation, a 3-D scatterplot should be examined to assess the relationship between focal variables within interval of scores on the control variable. As best as we can tell, the relationship between Interest and Accuracy appears weak, controlling for Latency.

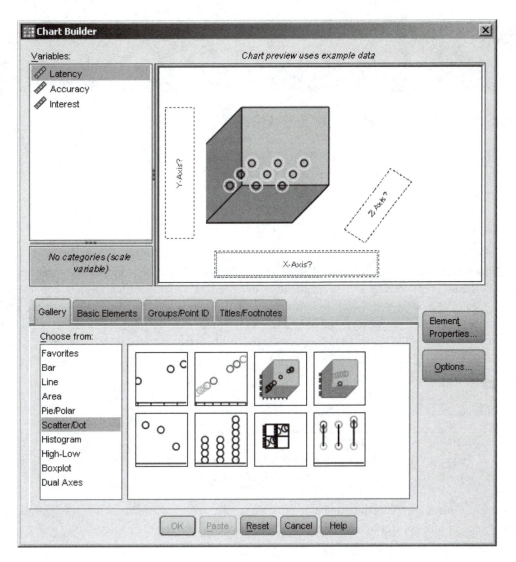

Figure 28.3 Selection of a simple 3-D scatterplot in the *Chart Builder* dialog box.

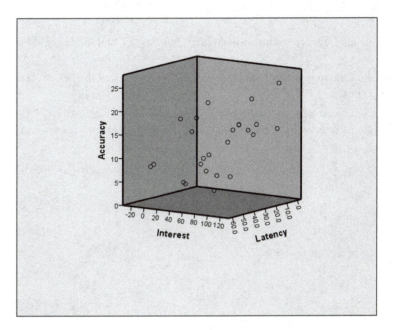

Figure 28.4 Simple 3-D scatterplot.

QuickStart 29 | Bivariate Linear Regression

Bivariate linear regression assesses the prediction of a quantitative dependent variable from an independent variable. We focus on predicting with a quantitative independent variable, although it is possible to use a qualitative predictor as well. An *F* test evaluates the null hypothesis that the dependent variable cannot be predicted linearly from the independent variable in the population. A scatterplot is created to develop a more complete understanding of the relationship between the independent and the dependent variables.

The Data

Our example data are in the file named Q29.sav.

Variable	Description
Training_X	Average number of hours per week of weight training
Injuries_Y	Number of days with injuries per season

In our example, a researcher is interested in predicting the number of days with injuries for college quarterbacks from the amount of time spent weight training. He is able to obtain data for 30 quarterbacks.

Conducting a Bivariate Linear Regression

1. Click *Analyze → Regression → Linear,* and you will see the *Linear Regression* dialog box, as shown in Figure 29.1.
2. Click on the name of the dependent variable (e.g., *Injuries_Y*), and then click ⬇ to move it to the *Dependent* box.
3. Click the name of the independent variable (e.g., *Training_X*), and then click ⬇ to move it to the *Independent(s)* box.
4. Click *Statistics* and you will see the *Linear Regression: Statistics* dialog box. *Put a check in the box next to Estimates, Confidence Intervals, Model Fit, and Descriptives*, as shown in Figure 29.2.
5. Click *Continue.*
6. Click *OK*, and you will see the partial results of the regression analysis, as shown in Figure 29.3.

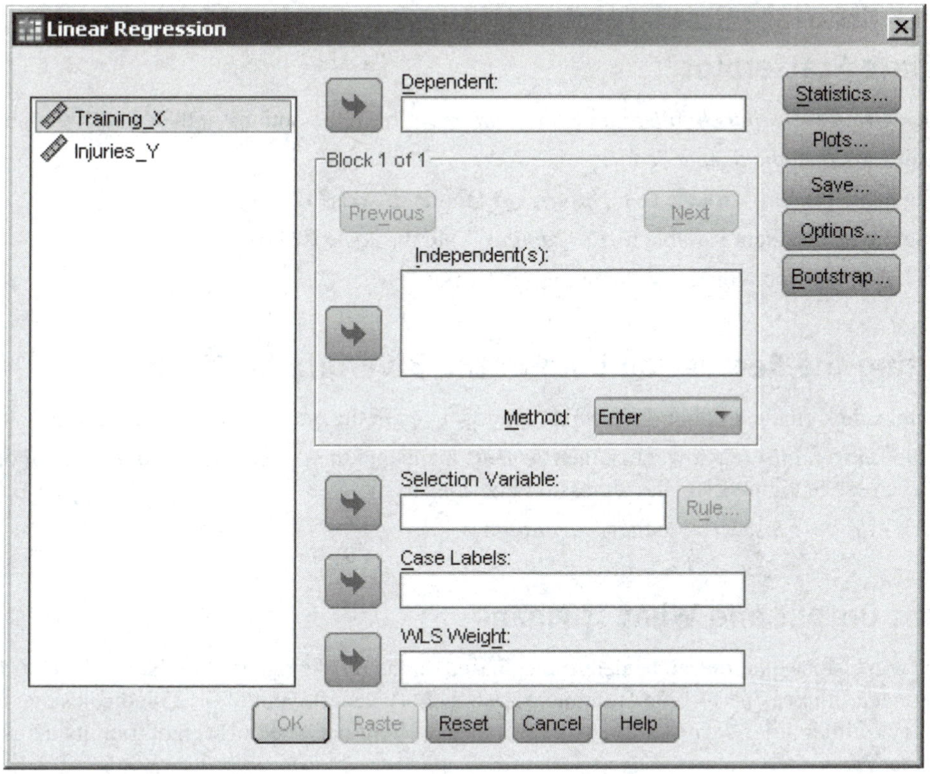

Figure 29.1 *Linear Regression* dialog box.

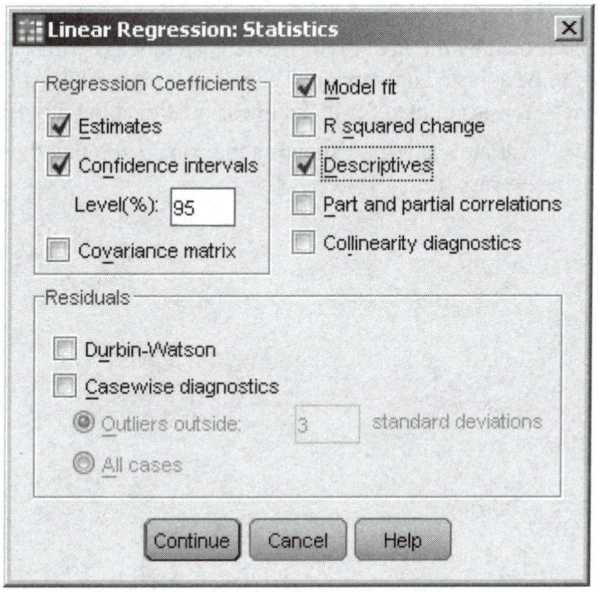

Figure 29.2 *Linear Regression: Statistics* dialog box.

Creating a Bivariate Scatterplot with the Regression Line
Bivariate Scatterplot

1. Click *Graphs* → *Chart Builder* and click *Scatter/Dot* from the options in the *Choose from* box.
2. Double click on the *Simple Scatter* icon.
3. Drag the dependent variable (e.g., *Injuries_Y*) to the Y-Axis? box.
4. Drag the independent variable (e.g., *Training_X*) to the X-Axis? box.
5. Click *OK*, and you will see the bivariate scatterplot.

Inserting the Regression Line in the Bivariate Scatterplot

1. Double click on the graph in the *Output* window to open the graph in the *Chart Editor*.
2. In the *Chart Editor* window, click the *Elements* menu and then select the *Fit Line at Total* option. As you can see in Figure 29.4, the regression line appears.
3. Click *Files* → *Close* to close the *Chart Editor*.

Important Output and What It Means

- The regression equation can be determined based on the results reported in the *Coefficients* table: Predicted Injuries_Y = −.125 (Training_X) + 6.847. The coefficient of −.125 indicates that the number of days with injuries decreases .125 days for every 1 hour per week of weight training across quarterbacks.

- The confidence interval for the −.125 coefficient is wide, ranging from −.219 to −.031. The interval does not contain the value of zero, indicating the hypothesis that weight training is not linearly related to injuries in the population can be rejected. The same hypothesis is evaluated with the F test, $F(1, 28) = 7.436$, $p = .011$.

- The effect size is represented by the R^2 of .210. The R^2 is an upwardly biased estimate of the population effect size and needs to be adjusted downward. The adjusted R^2 is .182. Approximately 18 percent of the variance of Injuries_Y is accounted for by its linear relationship with Training_X.

- An examination of the bivariate scatterplot supports the conclusion that there is a moderate negative linear relationship between variables.

Model Summary

Model	R	R Square	Adjusted R Square	Std. Error of the Estimate
1	.458[a]	.210	.182	2.182

a. Predictors: (Constant), Training_X

ANOVA[b]

Model		Sum of Squares	df	Mean Square	F	Sig.
1	Regression	35.395	1	35.395	7.436	.011[a]
	Residual	133.271	28	4.760		
	Total	168.667	29			

a. Predictors: (Constant), Training_X

b. Dependent Variable: Injuries_Y

Coefficients[a]

Model		Unstandardized Coefficients		Standardized Coefficients	t	Sig.	95.0% Confidence Interval for B	
		B	Std. Error	Beta			Lower Bound	Upper Bound
1	(Constant)	6.847	1.004		6.818	.000	4.790	8.904
	Training_X	-.125	.046	-.458	-2.727	.011	-.219	-.031

a. Dependent Variable: Injuries_Y

Figure 29.3 Partial results of the bivariate linear regression analysis.

Graph

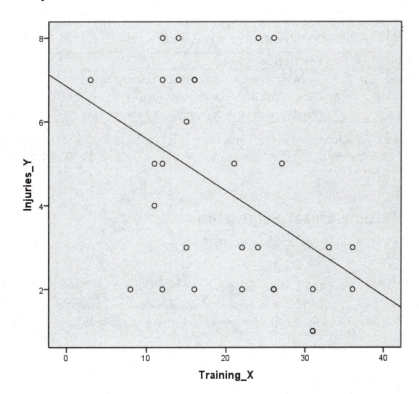

Figure 29.4 Scatterplot with regression line.

QuickStart 30 | Multiple Linear Regression

Multiple linear regression assesses the prediction of a quantitative dependent variable from multiple independent variables. We focus on predicting with quantitative independent variables, although one can use qualitative predictors. The F test for linear regression with multiple predictors evaluates the null hypothesis that the dependent variable cannot be predicted from the multiple independent variables linearly in the population. Researchers who conduct multiple linear regression analyses may be interested not only in the useful of the predictors as a group, but also the relative usefulness of the individual predictors. We have concentrated our efforts on the former.

Scatterplots can also be created to develop a more complete understanding of the relationship between the predictors and the dependent variable. At a minimum, bivariate scatterplots (see QuickStart 29) should be created between each predictor and the dependent variable. Additional plots can be created by clicking on the *Plots* button in the *Linear Regression* dialog box.

The Data

Our example data are in the file named Q30.sav.

Variables	Description
Training_X1	Mean hours per week of weight training
Stretching_X2	Mean hours per week of stretching
Injuries_Y	Number of days with injuries per season

In our example, a researcher is interested in predicting the number of days with injuries for college quarterbacks from the amount of time weight training and the amount of time stretching. He is able to obtain data for 30 quarterbacks.

Conducing a Multiple Linear Regression

1. Click *Analyze → Regression → Linear*, and you will see the *Linear Regression* dialog box as shown in Figure 30.1.
2. Click on the dependent variable (e.g., *Injuries_Y*) and then click ⊡ to move it to the *Dependent* box.
3. Holding down the Ctrl key, click on the independent variables (e.g., Training_X1 and Stretching_X2), and then click ⊡ to move them to the *Independents* box as you see in Figure 30.2.

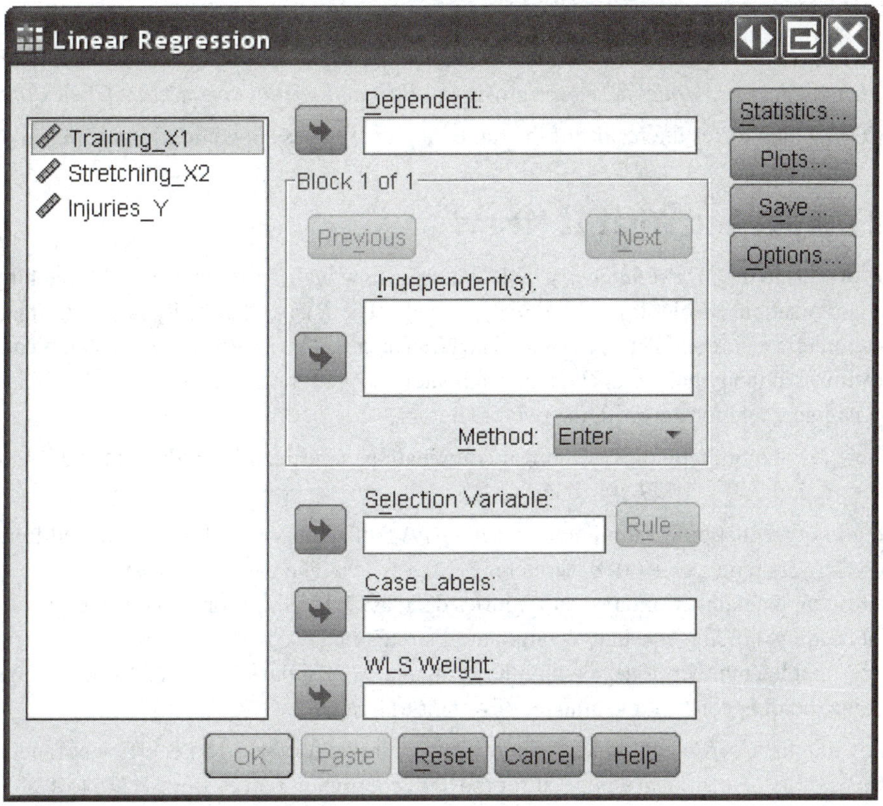

Figure 30.1 *Linear Regression* dialog box.

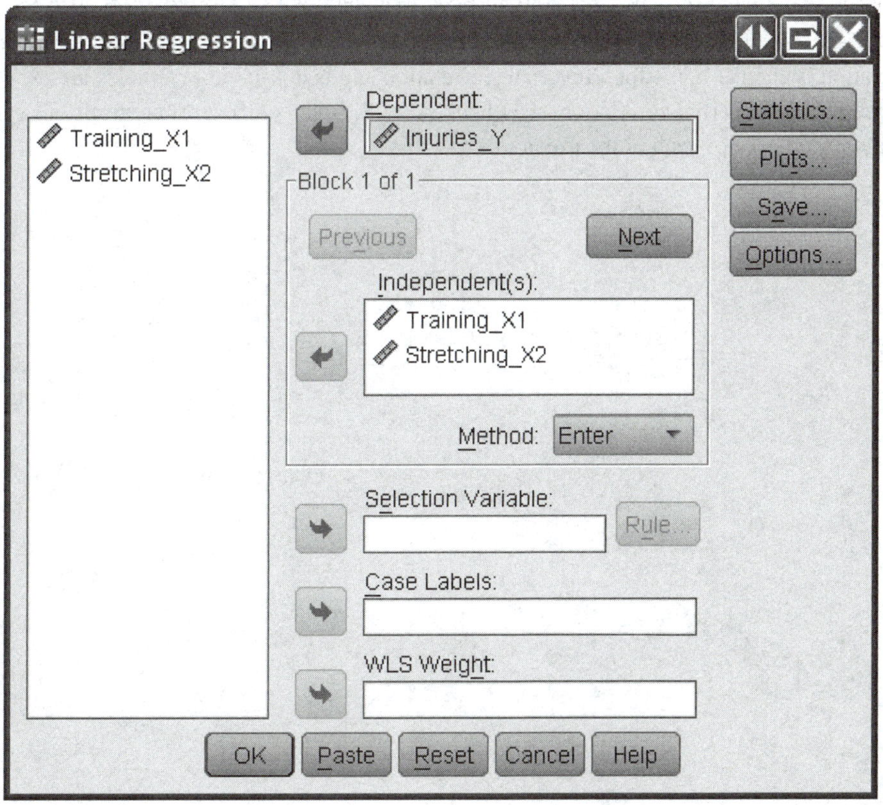

Figure 30.2 Completed *Linear Regression* dialog box.

4. Click *Statistics* and you will see the *Linear Regression: Statistics* dialog box. Click *Estimates, Confidence Intervals, Model fit, Descriptives* and *Part and partial correlation*. Click *Continue*.

5. Click *OK*. You will see the results of the regression analysis as shown in Figures 30.3 and 30.4.

Important Output and What It Means

- The R^2 of .218 in the *Model Summary* table indicates how well Training_X1 and Stretching_X2, in linear combination, predict Injuries_Y in the sample. The R^2 is an upwardly biased estimate of the population effect size and needs to be adjusted downward. The adjusted R^2 of .160 indicates that our best estimate in the population is that approximately 16% of the variance of Injuries_Y is accounted for by its linear relationship with the two predictors.

- Training_X1 and Stretching_X2, in linear combination, significantly predict at the .05 level Injuries_Y, $F(2, 27) = 3.759$, $p = .036$.

- The regression equation is found in the *Coefficients* table and is as follows: Predicted Injuries_ Y = (–.155) Training_X1 + (.078) Stretching_X2 + 6.811. The partial regression coefficient of –.155 indicates that the number of days with injuries decreases .155 days for every 1 hour per week of weight training, holding constant the amount of stretching. The partial regression coefficient of .078 indicates that the number of days with injuries increases .078 days for every 1 hour per week of stretching, holding constant the amount of weight training.

- As shown in the *Coefficients* table, the confidence interval for the –.155 coefficient ranges from –.308 to –.003, while the confidence interval for the .078 coefficient ranges from –.228 to +.385. Both interval are quite wide. Note the confidence interval for the partial regression coefficient for Stretching_X2 contains the value of zero. These results indicate the hypothesis cannot be rejected at the .05 level that stretching, holding weight training constant, is not linearly related to the number of injuries in the population. The same hypothesis is evaluated with a *t* test, $t(27) = .524$, $p = .604$.

- The *Coefficients* table also presents results for zero-order and partial correlations. A zero-order correlation is another name for a bivariate correlation and is discussed in QuickStart 27. For interpretation of a partial correlation, see QuickStart 28. Both coefficients are useful in interpreting the relative importance of each of the predictors.

Model Summary

Model	R	R Square	Adjusted R Square	Std. Error of the Estimate
1	.467[a]	.218	.160	2.210

a. Predictors: (Constant), Stretching_X2, Training_X1

ANOVA[b]

Model		Sum of Squares	df	Mean Square	F	Sig.
1	Regression	36.739	2	18.369	3.759	.036[a]
	Residual	131.928	27	4.886		
	Total	168.667	29			

a. Predictors: (Constant), Stretching_X2, Training_X1

b. Dependent Variable: Injuries_Y

Figure 30.3 Partial results of the multiple linear regression analysis.

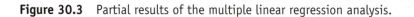

Coefficients[a]

Model		Unstandardized Coefficients		Standardized Coefficients			95.0% Confidence Interval for B		Correlations		
		B	Std. Error	Beta	t	Sig.	Lower Bound	Upper Bound	Zero-order	Partial	Part
1	(Constant)	6.811	1.020		6.679	.000	4.719	8.904			
	Training_X1	-.155	.074	-.569	-2.095	.046	-.308	-.003	-.458	-.374	-.357
	Stretching_X2	.078	.149	.142	.524	.604	-.228	.385	-.301	.100	.089

a. Dependent Variable: Injuries_Y

Figure 30.4 Partial results of the multiple linear regression analysis.

PART VIII

QuickStart 31 | Discriminant Analysis

Discriminant analysis assesses the prediction of a qualitative outcome variable from a set of quantitative predictor variables. The qualitative outcome variable is the grouping variable, and the quantitative predictor variables are independent variables. Discriminant functions are created that (a) are linear combinations of the independent variables, (b) maximize differences between groups, and (c) are uncorrelated with each other. Chi square (X^2) tests evaluate null hypotheses that discriminant functions are not useful in predicting the grouping variable in the population.

The Data

Our example data are in the file Q31.sav.

Variable	Description
Preparation	Assessment of skills in food preparation
Attractiveness	Assessment of skills in creating attractive plates of food
Taste	Assessment of taste of prepared food
Job_Ambition	Judged ambition to do well in the job market
Restaurant_Ambition	Judged ambition to do well in the restaurant business
Job_Outcome	1 = No longer working in restaurant business
	2 = Working in a routine restaurant position
	3 = Head chef at an independent restaurant

The first five variables were assessments by teachers of students who were attending a culinary school. The school then followed up five years later to determine their success in the restaurant business.

Performing a Discriminant Analysis

1. Click *Analyze → Classify → Discriminant,* and you will see the *Discriminant Analysis* dialog box as shown in Figure 31.1.

2. Click on the name of your grouping variable (e.g., *Job_Outcome*), and then click ⬛ to move it to the *Grouping Variable* box.

3. Click the *Define Range* button (see Figure 31.2), and type the minimum (e.g., 1) and maximum (e.g., 3) values on the *Grouping Variable*. Click *Continue.*

4. Holding down the Ctrl key, click on the names of your independent variables (e.g., *Preparation, Attractiveness, Taste, Job_Ambition,* and *Restaurant_Ambition*), and then click ⬛ to move them to the *Independents* box.

5. Click *Statistics* and you will see the *Discriminant Analysis: Statistics* dialog box, as shown in Figure 31.3. Click the following options (at a minimum): *Means, Univariate ANOVAs, and Within-groups correlation.* Click *Continue.*

6. Click *Classify,* and you will see the *Discriminant Analysis: Classification* dialog box, as shown in Figure 31.4. You should make choices based on your understanding of your data. We chose *Compute from group sizes, Within-groups, Summary Table,* and *Leave-one-out classification* for our example. Click *Continue.*

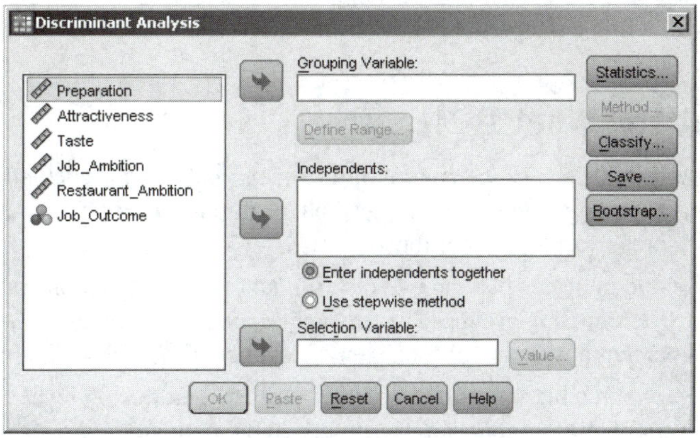

Figure 31.1 *Discriminant Analysis* dialog box.

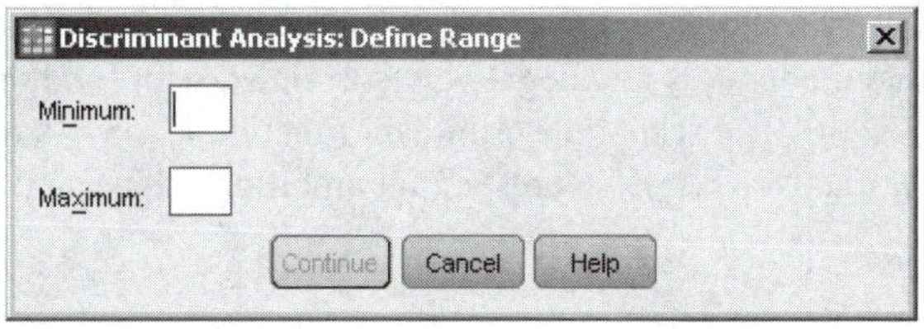

Figure 31.2 *Discriminant Analysis: Define Range* dialog box.

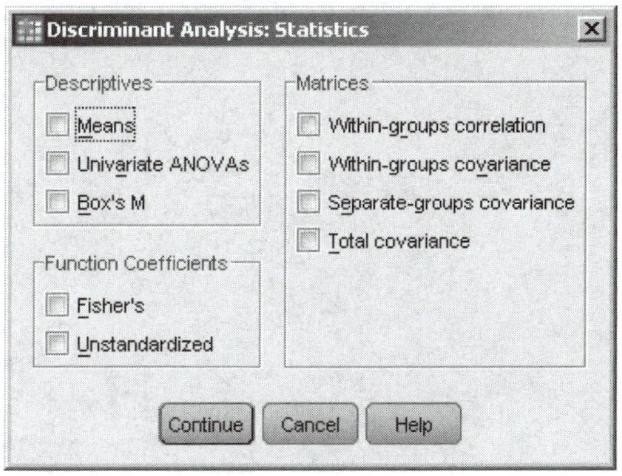

Figure 31.3 *Discriminant Analysis: Statistics* dialog box.

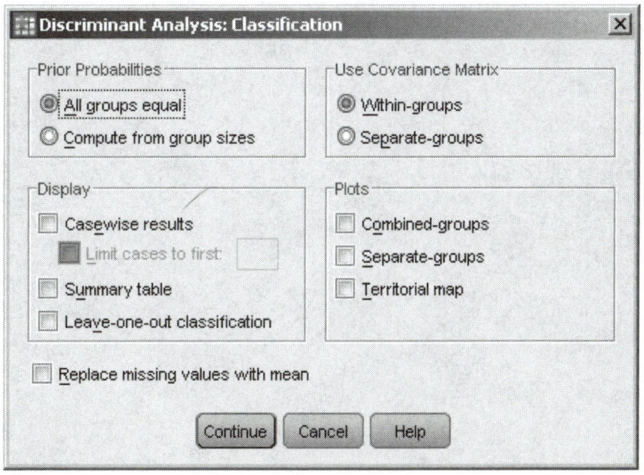

Figure 31.4 *Discriminant Analysis: Classification* dialog box.

7. Click *OK,* and you will see the partial results of the analysis in Figure 31.5 and Figure 31.6.

Important Output and What It Means

- The *Group Statistics* table shows the pattern of the means and standard deviations across the three job-outcome groups. One interesting result was head chefs at independent restaurants were on average higher on all measures except job ambition.

- The *Eigenvalues* table indicates that the two discriminant functions demonstrate approximately the same strength in differentiating groups. The first and second eigenvalues (i.e., .359 and .298) are 54.6 percent and 45.4 percent of the sum of the eigenvalues (i.e., .657), respectively.

- From the *Wilks' Lambda* table, the null hypothesis is rejected at the .05 level that the discriminant functions as a set cannot differentiate among groups in the population, $X^2(10, N = 50) = 25.558$, $p = .004$. We can also reject the null hypothesis that the remaining functions (in our example, the second discriminant function) cannot differentiate among groups in the population, $X^2(4, N = 50) = 11.750$, $p = .019$.

- Based on the *Structure Matrix*, the first discriminant function is strongly and positively correlated with job ambition (.711) and moderately and negatively correlated with food preparation (–.442) and restaurant ambition (–.414). The second discriminant function is fairly strongly and positively correlated with food attractiveness (.571), restaurant ambition (.548), and food taste (.531).

Eigenvalues

Function	Eigenvalue	% of Variance	Cumulative %	Canonical Correlation
1	.359[a]	54.6	54.6	.514
2	.298[a]	45.4	100.0	.479

a. First 2 canonical discriminant functions were used in the analysis.

Wilks' Lambda

Test of Function(s)	Wilks' Lambda	Chi-square	df	Sig.
1 through 2	.567	25.558	10	.004
2	.770	11.750	4	.019

Structure Matrix

	Function	
	1	2
Job_Ambition	.711[*]	.287
Preparation	-.442[*]	.282
Attractiveness	-.134	.571[*]
Restaurant_Ambition	-.414	.548[*]
Taste	-.090	.531[*]

Pooled within-groups correlations between discriminating variables and standardized canonical discriminant functions
Variables ordered by absolute size of correlation within function.

[*]. Largest absolute correlation between each variable and any discriminant function

Functions at Group Centroids

Job_Outcome	Function	
	1	2
No longer works in restaurant business	.931	-.033
Working in a routine restaurant position	-.375	-.294
Head chef at an independent restaurant	-.308	1.282

Unstandardized canonical discriminant functions evaluated at group means

Figure 31.5 Partial results of the discriminant analysis.

- The *Functions at Group Centroids* table gives the means on the discriminant functions. The first discriminant function appears to differentiate graduates who are still in the restaurant business versus those who are not. The second discriminant function seems to differentiate graduates who are head chefs at independent restaurants from other graduates.

- Overall, we conclude that graduates who were ambitious in terms of jobs, but less ambitious in terms of working in the restaurant industry tended not to work in the restaurant business at the end of five years. Also, graduates who had high aspirations in the restaurant business and could prepare tasty, well presented food were more likely to become chefs in independent restaurants.

- The *Classification Results* table shows that 70.0 percent of the graduates were correctly classified in the sample based on the predictor variables. However, this classification rate is too high in terms of predicting graduates in general. A better prediction rate is 60.0 percent.

Classification Results[b],[c]

	Job_Outcome		Predicted Group Membership			
			No longer works in restaurant business	Working in a routine restaurant position	Head chef at an independent restaurant	Total
Original	Count	No longer works in restaurant business	8	5	1	14
		Working in a routine restaurant position	4	24	1	29
		Head chef at an independent restaurant	1	3	3	7
	%	No longer works in restaurant business	57.1	35.7	7.1	100.0
		Working in a routine restaurant position	13.8	82.8	3.4	100.0
		Head chef at an independent restaurant	14.3	42.9	42.9	100.0
Cross-validated[a]	Count	No longer works in restaurant business	7	6	1	14
		Working in a routine restaurant position	7	21	1	29
		Head chef at an independent restaurant	1	4	2	7
	%	No longer works in restaurant business	50.0	42.9	7.1	100.0
		Working in a routine restaurant position	24.1	72.4	3.4	100.0
		Head chef at an independent restaurant	14.3	57.1	28.6	100.0

a. Cross validation is done only for those cases in the analysis. In cross validation, each case is classified by the functions derived from all cases other than that case.

b. 70.0% of original grouped cases correctly classified.

c. 60.0% of cross-validated grouped cases correctly classified.

Figure 31.6   Partial results of the discriminant analysis.

Factor analysis is applied to assess the dimensions underlying a set of variables and involves two phases. The goal of the first phase is to determine the number of factors. We strongly discourage the use of the default option to determine the number of factors (the eigenvalues-greater-than-one criterion) because of its inaccuracy and instead, support the use of scree plots as well as the interpretability of factors. SPSS assumes users will determine the number of factors using principal components, regardless of the chosen extraction method. The second phase involves rotating the factors to make them more interpretable. Typically substantive theory about the constructs underlying a set of measures dictates correlated factors. Accordingly, users should use oblique (e.g., direct oblimin) rather than orthogonal (e.g., Varimax) rotational methods in most applications. In the second phase, we recommend using principal axis to extract factors because other methods tend to be more problematic.

The Data

Our example data is in the file Q32.sav.

Variables	Definition
V1 to V5	Scales assess degree to which women watch baseball (V1), basketball (V2), football (V3), tennis (V4), and golf (V5) on television.
V6 to V10	Scales assess degree to which women watch dramas (V6), situational comedies (V7), reality shows (V8), talk shows (V9), and food shows (V10) on television.

In our example, a researcher wants to determine the dimensions underlying a set of 10 scales that assess the degree to which women watch various types of television programs. The scales are described in the table. She collects data on these scales from 200 women.

Performing Factor Analysis

We conduct the factor analysis in two phases.

Phase 1: Determining the Number of Factors

1. Click *Analyze → Dimension Reduction → Factor*, and you will see the *Factor Analysis* dialog box as shown in Figure 32.1.

2. Press the *Ctrl + A key* combination to select all the variables in the list and then click ⬛ to move the variables to the *Variables* box.

3. Click *Extraction* and you will see the *Factor Analysis: Extraction* dialog box as shown in Figure 32.2.
   a. Choose the default option *Principal Components* from the drop down menu under *Method* because SPSS uses this method to create scree plots regardless of user's choice of method.
   b. Click *Unrotated factor solution* and *Scree Plot*. Click *Continue*.

4. Click *OK*, and you will see the results of the extraction in Figures 32.3 and 32.4.

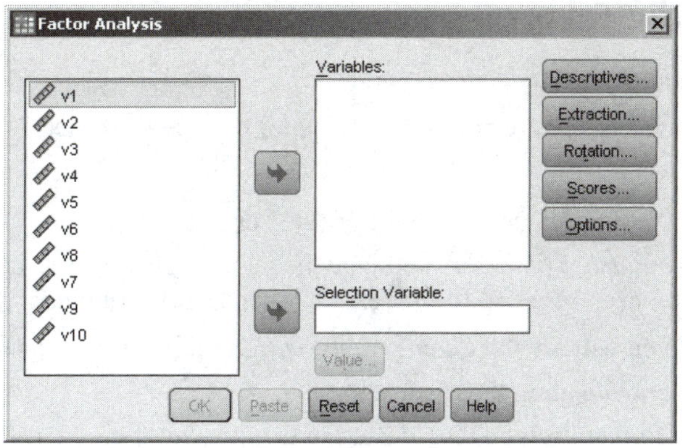

Figure 32.1 *Factor Analysis* dialog box.

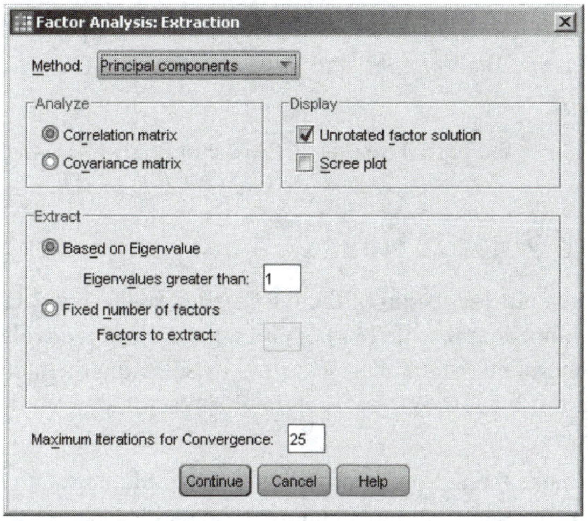

Figure 32.2 *Factor Analysis Extraction* dialog box.

Communalities

	Initial	Extraction
v1	1.000	.675
v2	1.000	.708
v3	1.000	.729
v4	1.000	.715
v5	1.000	.666
v6	1.000	.732
v8	1.000	.679
v7	1.000	.766
v9	1.000	.734
v10	1.000	.719

Extraction Method: Principal
Component Analysis.

Total Variance Explained

Component	Initial Eigenvalues			Extraction Sums of Squared Loadings		
	Total	% of Variance	Cumulative %	Total	% of Variance	Cumulative %
1	4.603	46.029	46.029	4.603	46.029	46.029
2	2.521	25.206	71.235	2.521	25.206	71.235
3	.529	5.288	76.523			
4	.415	4.149	80.672			
5	.388	3.878	84.550			
6	.384	3.841	88.391			
7	.333	3.333	91.724			
8	.301	3.005	94.729			
9	.267	2.673	97.403			
10	.260	2.597	100.000			

Extraction Method: Principal Component Analysis.

Figure 32.3 Output showing *Total Variance Explained* table.

Phase 2: Rotating the Factors

1. Click *Analyze → Dimension Reduction → Factor.*

2. If the variables to be analyzed are not in the *Variables* box, perform step 2 in Phase 1.

3. Click *Extraction.*

   a. Click *Principal axis factoring* in the *Method* drop down menu.

   b. Click *Fixed number of factors* and type the number of factors to be extracted based on your decision in Phase 1 (e.g., 2 for our example) and click *Continue.*

4. Click *Rotation* and you will see the *Factor Analysis: Rotation* dialog box as shown in Figure 32.5.

   a. Click *Direct Oblimin* in the *Method* area.

   b. Make sure *Rotated solution* is selected in the *Display* area.

   c. Click *Continue.*

5. Click *Descriptives*

   a. Click *Univariate descriptives* in the *Statistics* area.

   b. Click *Coefficients, Determinant,* and *Reproduced* in the *Correlation Matrix* area.

   c. Click *Continue.*

6. Click *OK,* and you will see the partial results of the factor analysis as shown in Figure 32.6.

Important Output and What It Means

- The scree plot is a visual representation of the information in the *Total Variance Explained* table. The values in the *Total* column are presented in the plot and labeled eigenvalues (i.e., the factor variances). Users of scree plots determine the number of factors by selecting the factors that occur prior to the perceived "elbow." In this case, the elbow is at the third factor so we retain the factors prior to this point, that is, two factors.

- Factors are rotated to make them more interpretable. If an oblique rotation is used, three matrices should be examined before interpreting and naming the factors:

   o *Pattern Matrix*: It contains the coefficients applied to the factors to predict the scales. These coefficients are similar to partial regression coefficients. For example, the coefficients for F1 and F2 are .053 and .753, respectively, in predicting V1. The first five variables associated with sports programs is primarily a function of the second factor, while the second five variables are largely a function of the first factor. Based on these results, we might name the first factor, Watching Sports on TV, and the second factor, Watching Non-Sports Programs on TV.

   o *Factor Correlation Matrix*: It contains the correlation between the two factors. In our example, the correlation of .320 is moderate in size.

   o *Structure Matrix*: It contains the correlations between the variables and the factors. Because the two factors are moderately correlated, the first scale (Watching Baseball) is not only correlated strongly (i.e., .770) with factor 2, named Watching Sports on TV, but also moderately (i.e., .294) with factor 1, Watching Non-Sports Programs on TV.

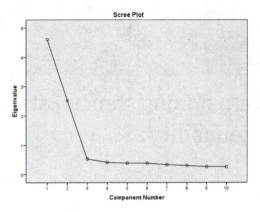

Figure 32.4 Scree plot.

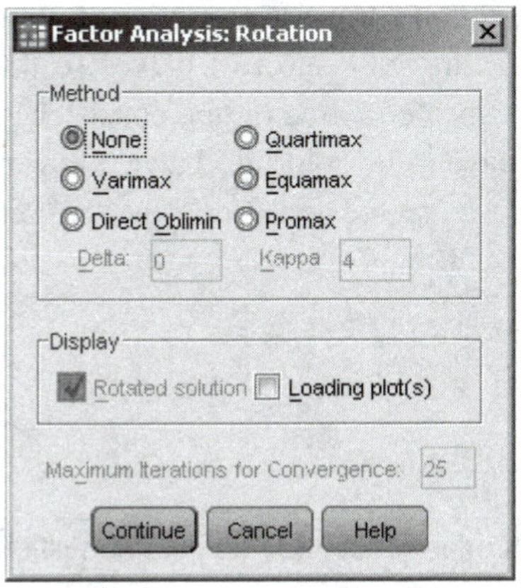

Figure 32.5 *Factor Analysis: Rotation* dialog box.

Pattern Matrix[a]

	Factor 1	Factor 2
v1	.053	.753
v2	-.014	.801
v3	-.031	.826
v4	.038	.794
v5	-.032	.765
v6	.800	.051
v8	.770	-.010
v7	.865	-.064
v9	.808	.035
v10	.803	.000

Structure Matrix

	Factor 1	Factor 2
v1	.294	.770
v2	.242	.797
v3	.233	.816
v4	.292	.806
v5	.213	.755
v6	.816	.307
v8	.767	.236
v7	.844	.213
v9	.819	.294
v10	.803	.257

Factor Correlation Matrix

Factor	1	2
1	1.000	.320
2	.320	1.000

Figure 32.6 Partial results of the rotated factors.

Internal Consistency Estimates of Reliability

A reliability coefficient indicates whether a measure yields consistent scores and can be computed using a variety of methods. We focus on two internal consistency methods: the split-half coefficient and coefficient alpha. For a split-half coefficient, items are split into two halves so that the two halves are as equivalent as possible, and reliability estimates are computed based on the consistency between scores on the half tests. For coefficient alpha, a measure does not have to be split into halves; however, it requires items to be equivalent. Coefficient alpha estimates reliability based on the consistency in item scores.

The Data

Our example data are in file Q33.sav.

Variable	Definition
Item1	In comparison with other students, I do best on tests that are hard to complete on time.
Item2	I enjoy the challenge of tests that have to be completed in a short time period.
Item3	It feels good to be one of the early finishers of tests.
Item4	I tend to complete tests early.
Item5	On essay exams, I give direct answers with little elaboration.
Item6	I dislike tests that take a long time to finish.
Item7	When I review my answers on tests, I frequently change answers that were correct.
Item8	I become more confused the longer I think about test questions.
Item9	I trust my first responses to test items.
Item10	I like tests where speed counts in my favor.

A researcher developed the Speed in Finishing Tests (SIFT) scale consisting of 10 items. Thirty five students responded to items on a five-point scale to assess its reliability using coefficient alpha and a split-half reliability coefficient. For the split half coefficient, he splits the test so the odd-numbered items are on one half and the even-numbered items are on the other half.

Computing Coefficient Alpha

1. Click *Analyze → Scale → Reliability Analysis*, and you will see the *Reliability Analysis* dialog box as shown in Figure 33.1.
2. Holding down the Ctrl key, click on the names of your items (e.g., Item1 through Item10), and then click ⬇ to move them to the *Items* box. Click *Alpha* from the *Model* drop down menu.
3. Click *Statistics*, and you will see the *Reliability Analysis: Statistics* dialog box as shown in Figure 33.2.

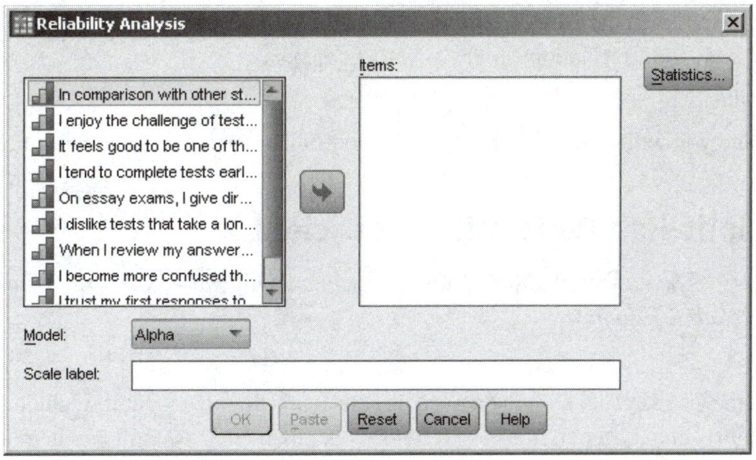

Figure 33.1 *Reliability Analysis* dialog box.

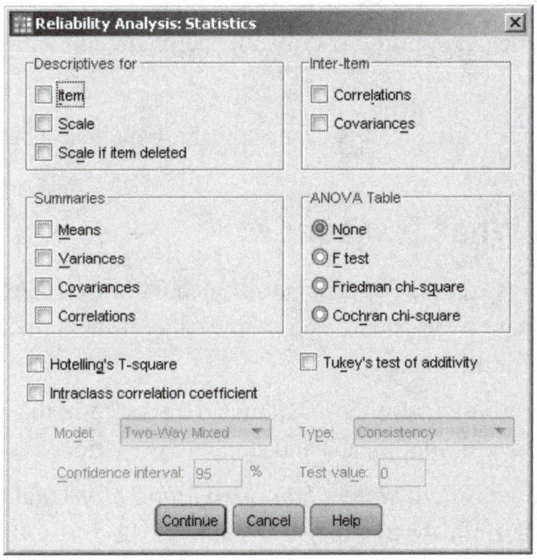

Figure 33.2 *Reliability Analysis: Statistics* dialog box.

4. Click *Item* and *Scale* in the *Descriptives for* area; *Means, Variances,* and *Correlations* in the *Summaries* area; and Correlations in the *Inter-Item* area.

5. Click *Continue*.

6. Click *OK*, and you will see partial results of the coefficient analysis as shown in Figure 33.3.

Computing a Split-Half Reliability Coefficient

1. Click *Analyze* → *Scale* → *Reliability Analysis* or click the *Recall recently used dialogs* on the Toolbar and select *Reliability Analysis*.

2. Click *Reset*.

3. Hold down the Ctrl key, click on the names of your items that you want to include on one half of the test (e.g., Item1, Item3, Item5, Item7, and Item9), and then click 🔽 to move them to the *Items* box.

4. Hold down the *Ctrl* key, click on the names of your items that you want to include on the other half of the test (e.g., Item2 , Item4, Item6, Item8, and Item10), and then click 🔽 to move them to the *Items* box.

5. Click *Split-half* from the *Model* drop down menu.

6. Click *Statistics* and choose the options described in step 5 under Computing Coefficient Alpha.

7. Click Continue.

8. Click *OK*, and you will see partial results of the split-half analysis as shown in Figure 33.4.

Important Output and What It Means

- You are most likely interested in the coefficient labeled Cronbach's Alpha. In this case it is .927. The other coefficient alpha (e.g., .929) should be reported only if the items are standardized prior to computing a total score for the scale.

- The mean and standard deviations for the 10 items are reported in the *Item Statistics* table. Based on these results, the items have similar means and standard deviations.

- The correlations among items in the *Inter-Item Correlation Matrix* table are generally moderate to strong, with most ranging from .40 to .70.

- Descriptive statistics (e.g., mean) of the item means, variances, and correlations are reported in the *Summary Item Statistics* table.

- If coefficient alpha is computed, it is assumed that a scale score for a respondent is the sum of item scores. Descriptive statistics for the scale scores are reported in the *Scale Statistics* table.

- The correlation between forms (i.e., halves) is .758, but it is not a reliability estimate. The Spearman-Brown corrected correlation of .978 is the reliability estimate. The one labeled Unequal Length should be reported if the number of items differs between halves. To the extent that items are not equivalent, the split-half reliability coefficient may be greater than coefficient alpha, as it is for our example.

Reliability Statistics

Cronbach's Alpha	Cronbach's Alpha Based on Standardized Items	N of Items
.927	.929	10

Item Statistics

	Mean	Std. Deviation	N
In comparison with other students, I do best on tests that are hard to complete on time.	2.80	1.491	35
I enjoy the challenge of tests that have to be completed in a short time period.	3.31	1.255	35
It feels good to be one of the early finishers of tests.	3.37	1.165	35
I tend to complete tests early.	3.14	.912	35
On essay exams, I give direct answers with little elaboration.	3.14	1.089	35
I dislike tests that take a long time to finish.	3.26	1.291	35
When I review my answers on tests, I frequently change answers that were correct.	3.23	1.215	35
I become more confused the longer I think about test questions.	3.00	1.085	35
I trust my first responses to test items.	3.11	1.323	35
I like tests where speed counts in my favor.	3.20	1.410	35

Figure 33.3 Partial results for analyses to compute coefficient alpha.

Reliability Statistics

Cronbach's Alpha	Part 1	Value	.850
		N of Items	5[a]
	Part 2	Value	.840
		N of Items	5[b]
		Total N of Items	10
Correlation Between Forms			.956
Spearman-Brown Coefficient	Equal Length		.978
	Unequal Length		.978
Guttman Split-Half Coefficient			.977

Figure 33.4 Partial results for analyses to compute a split-half coefficient.

QuickStart 34 | # Binomial Test

The binomial test assesses hypotheses about a classification variable with two categories (e.g., gender). It evaluates whether the population proportion of individuals in one category (the first category specified in the data file) is equal to a hypothesized value (the default value being .50). The SPSS data file for this test may be structured two ways. With the standard method, the file contains the classification variable with as many cases as individuals. With the weighted cases method, the file contains two variables and two cases. The first variable is the categorical variable and includes its two values. The second variable includes the frequencies associated with each of the two values.

The Data

Our example data are in the file Q34.sav.

Variable	Definition
Gender_of_Listener	0 = Girl, 1 = Boy
Frequency	Number who chose each option

A researcher is interested in assessing whether 8-year-old girls would choose to discuss their problems with an 8-year-old girl or boy. She asks 115 girls to describe problems they are having. After describing their problems, the researcher states that frequently children can feel better about their problems if they talk to other children about them. The researcher then asks the girls if they would rather talk to an 8-year-old girl or boy about their problems. We will use the weighted cases method in the analysis of our example data.

Performing the Binomial Test with the Weighted Cases Method

1. Click *Data → Weight Cases*, and you will see the *Weight cases* dialog box, as shown in Figure 34.1.
2. Click *Weight cases by*.
3. Click the name of the variable representing the frequencies associated with the two categories (*Frequency* in this example) and move it to the *Frequency Variable* box. Click *OK*. The cases are now weighted in accord with the variable representing the frequencies for the two categories.

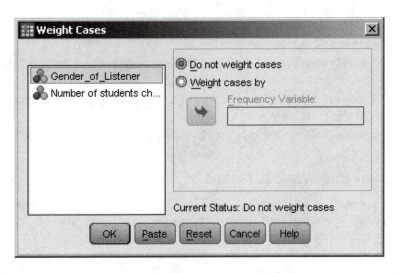

Figure 34.1 *Weight cases* dialog box.

4. Click *Analyze → Nonparametric Tests → Legacy Dialogs → Binomial*, and you will see the *Binomial Test* dialog box as shown in Figure 34.2.

5. Click the categorical variable (e.g., *Gender_of_Listener*), and then click ⬇ to move it to the *Test Variable List* box.

6. Choose the *Test proportion* of interest. For our example, we maintained the default option of 0.50 for the *Test Proportion*.

7. Click *OK*, and you will see the results of the binomial test as shown in Figure 34.3.

Important Output and What It Means

- The observed proportion of .74 indicates that 74 percent of the girls chose a girl as a listener. The sample proportion is substantially different from .50, that is, what one would expect if a very large number of research participants randomly chose the gender of a listener.

- We can reject at the .05 level the null hypothesis that the population proportion is equal to .50 in that the *p* value based on an approximate *z* test is less than .001.

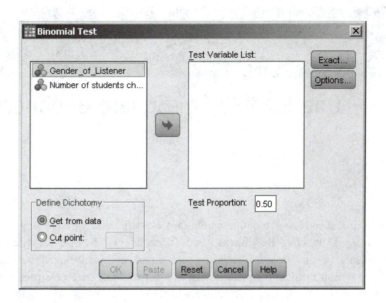

Figure 34.2 *Binomial Test* dialog box.

Binomial Test

		Category	N	Observed Prop.	Test Prop.	Asymp. Sig. (2-tailed)
Gender_of_Listener	Group 1	Girl listener	85	.74	.50	.000[a]
	Group 2	Boy listener	30	.26		
	Total		115	1.00		

a. Based on Z Approximation.

Figure 34.3 Results of binomial test.

A one-sample chi-square test evaluates hypotheses about a classification variable (e.g., political party) with multiple categories (e.g., Democrat, Republican, and Independent). It assesses whether the population proportions of individuals in the various categories are equal to hypothesized values, frequently equal proportions (the default option in SPSS). An SPSS data file for this test may be structured with the standard method, where the file contains the categorical variable with as many cases as individuals or with the weighted cases method, where the file contains two variables and as many cases as there are categories. The first variable is the categorical variable and includes a value for each of its categories. The second variable includes the frequencies associated with each of the values of the categorical variable.

The Data

Our example data are in the file Q35.sav.

Variable	Definition
Political_View	1 = Liberal, 2 = Conservative, 3 = Middle of the road

A researcher is interested in how new voters label themselves politically. He gains the cooperation of 50 new voters and asks them whether they see themselves politically as liberal, conservative, or middle of the road. He wishes to evaluate if new voters split themselves equally among the three choices. For our example, we analyze data that are in a file with a standard structure.

Performing the One Sample Chi-Square Goodness of Fit Test

1. Click *Analyze → Nonparametric Tests → Legacy Dialogs → Chi-square*, and you will see the *Chi-square Test* dialog box as shown in Figure 35.1.

2. Click on the name of your categorical variable (e.g., *Political_View*), and then click ⬇ to move it to the *Test Variable List* box.

3. If you have hypothesized equal population proportions, maintain the default option *All categories equal* in the *Expected Values* area. Otherwise, you must click on *Values* and type the expected value (hypothesized proportion X sample size) for each of the categories.

4. Click *OK*, and you will see the results of the chi-square analysis as shown in Figure 35.2.

Important Output and What It Means

- In our example, we hypothesized equal proportions, that is, .333 for the three categories of liberal, conservative, and middle of the road. An expected frequency is the hypothesized proportion X sample size. Accordingly, the expected frequency for each category is 16.7 = .333 X 50.

- We can reject at the .05 level the null hypothesis that population proportions are equal across the three categories, $X^2(2, N = 50) = 6.040, p = .049$.

- The X^2 test is approximate and may not be as accurate if some of the expected frequencies in the cells are less than 5.

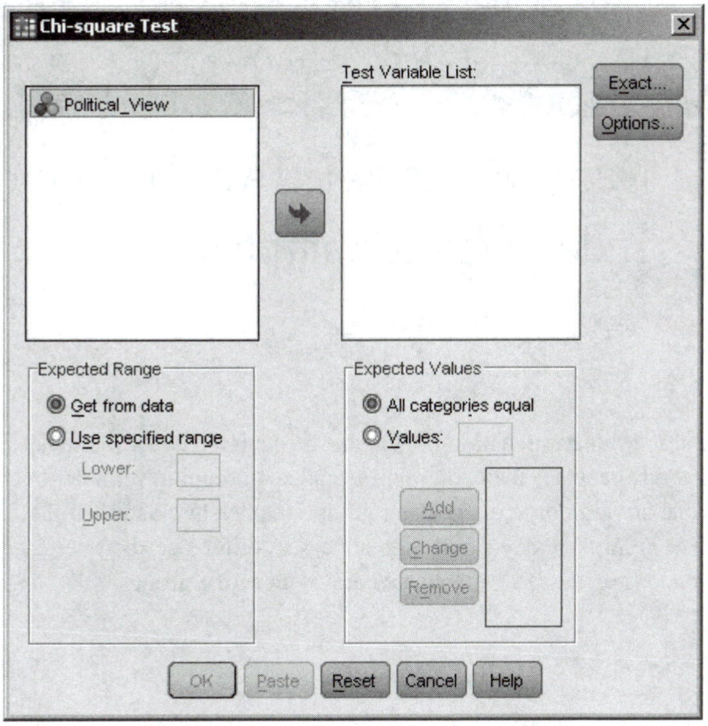

Figure 35.1 *Chi Square Test* dialog box.

Chi-Square Test

Political_View

	Observed N	Expected N	Residual
Liberal	18	16.7	1.3
Conservative	9	16.7	-7.7
Middle of the road	23	16.7	6.3
Total	50		

Test Statistics

	Political_View
Chi-square	6.040[a]
df	2
Asymp. Sig.	.049

Figure 35.2 Results of the chi-square analysis.

Mann-Whitney *U* Test for Two
Independent Samples

The Mann-Whitney *U* test evaluates whether population medians on a test variable are equal between two groups. The variable that differentiates the two groups is called a grouping variable. In conducting this test, the scores on the test variable are rank ordered ignoring group membership, and then the mean ranks for the two groups are compared. The Mann-Whitney *U* test does not assess differences between medians unless the shapes of the population distributions on the test variable are equivalent across groups.

The Data

Our example data are in the file Q36.sav.

Variable	Definition
friends_at_50	1 = Described self as having few close friends
	2 = Described self as having a number of close friends
age_died	Age of death

The researcher is interested in investigating whether people who live longer perceive themselves as having a circle of close friends. She has access to data from a questionnaire completed 60 years ago by 50 women. All women were 48 years old at the time they responded to the questionnaire. They were asked on the questionnaire which of the following two statements best described themselves: (1) I have few close friends or (2) I have a number of close friends. The researcher determined when each of these women died.

Performing the Mann-Whitney *U* Test

1. Click *Analyze → Nonparametric Tests → Legacy Dialogs → 2 Independent Samples*, and you will see the *Two-Independent-Samples Tests* dialog box as shown in Figure 36.1.

2. Click on the grouping variable (e.g., friends_at_50), and then click ⬇ to move it to the *Grouping Variable* box.

3. Click *Define Groups,* and you will see the *Two Independent Samples: Define Groups* dialog box as shown in Figure 36.2.

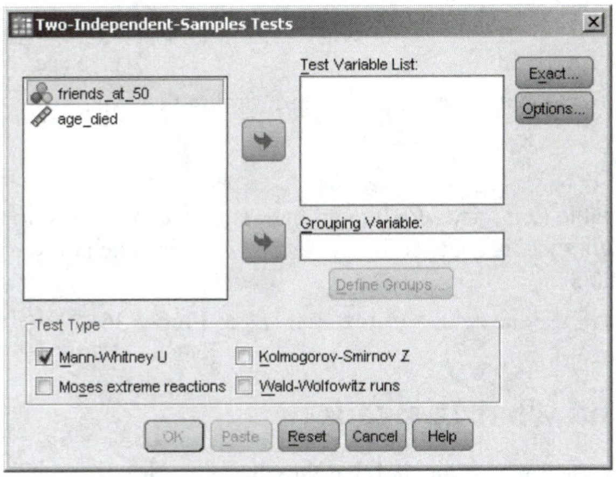

Figure 36.1 *Two-Independent-Samples Tests* dialog box.

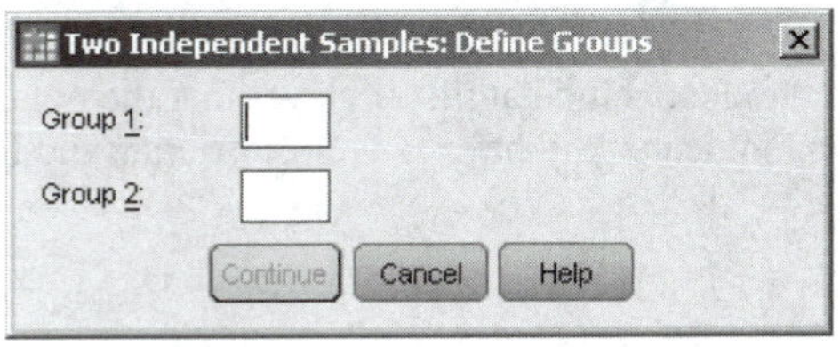

Figure 36.2 *Two Independent Samples: Define Groups* dialog box.

4. In the *Group 1* box, type the number (e.g., 1) representing one of the two values on the grouping variable in your data file.

5. In the *Group 2* box, type the number (e.g., 2) representing the other value on the grouping variable in your data file.

6. Click *Continue*.

7. Click on the test variable (e.g., *age_died*) , and then click ![button] to move it to the *Test Variable List* box. Make sure *Mann-Whitney U* is checked in the *Test Type* area. The complete dialog box should appear as shown in Figure 36.3.

8. Click *OK*, and you will see the results of the analysis in Figure 36.4.

Important Output and What It Means

- The mean rank for women who indicated that they had few close friends is 24.62, whereas the mean rank for women who indicated they had a number of close friends is 26.83.

- The difference in mean ranks of 2.21 suggests that in the sample, women who indicated they had a number of close friend tended to live longer. The difference in ranks of 2.21 is not substantial given the maximum rank is 50.

- Based on the results, we cannot conclude at the .05 level that the population age-of-death medians differ between women who indicate they have few close friends and those who state they have a number of close friends, $z = -.526$, $p = .599$.

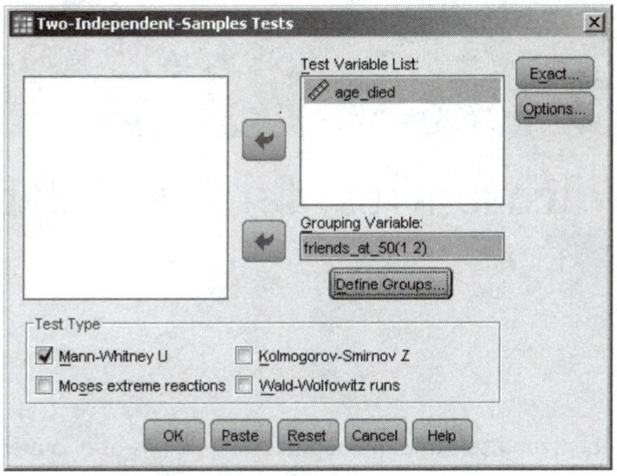

Figure 36.3   Completed Mann-Whitney *U* test dialog box.

Mann-Whitney Test

Ranks

	friends_at_50	N	Mean Rank	Sum of Ranks
age_died	Few	30	24.62	738.50
	A number	20	26.83	536.50
	Total	50		

Test Statistics[a]

	age_died
Mann-Whitney U	273.500
Wilcoxon W	738.500
Z	-.526
Asymp. Sig. (2-tailed)	.599

Figure 36.4   Results of the Mann-Whitney *U* test.

Wilcoxon Test for Two Related Samples

The Wilcoxon test evaluates the hypothesis that the population medians of two measures are equal to each other when the scores from these measures are paired. Scores may be paired because each research participant contributes a pair of scores (e.g., scores before and after participating in an intervention). Alternatively, scores may be paired because participants are sampled in pairs (e.g., husband-wife couples) or participants are treated as pairs in a study (e.g., boy-girl pairs in a cooperative learning study).

The Data

Our example data are in the file Q37.sav.

Variable	Definition
pre_hr	Scores on an empathy scale before training
post_hr	Scores on an empathy scale after training

A researcher is interested in assessing whether self-reported empathy changes when exposed to a human relationships training program. She has data from 35 men who watched a film on improving communication and expressing feelings. These men also wrote essays discussing the film and its meaning in terms of their own relationships. They completed an empathy scale before and after the training program.

Performing the Wilcoxon Test

1. Click *Analyze → Nonparametric Tests → Legacy Dialogs → 2 Related Samples*, and you will see the *Two-Related-Samples Tests* dialog box as shown in Figure 37.1.
2. Click on the first variable name in the pair (e.g., *pre_hr*) and then click 🔽 to move it to the *Variable1* location in the *Test Pairs* box. Alternatively, you can drag the variable name to the *Variable1* location.
3. Click on the second variable name in the pair (e.g., *post_hr*) and then click 🔽 to move it to the *Variable2* location in the *Test Pairs* box. Alternatively, you can drag the variable name to the *Variable2* location. The completed dialog box is shown in Figure 37.2.

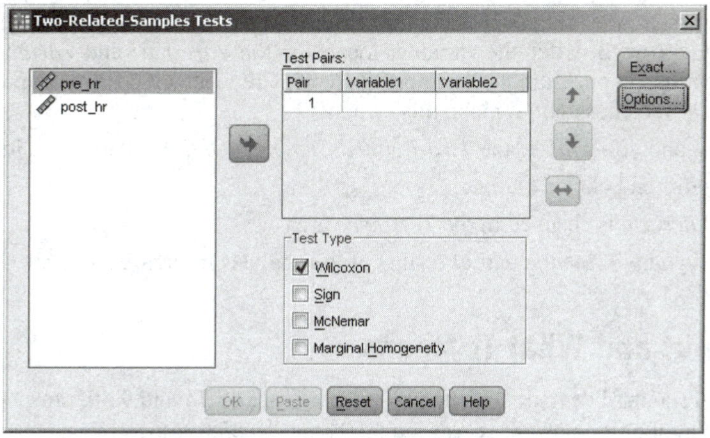

Figure 37.1 *Two-Related-Samples Tests* dialog box.

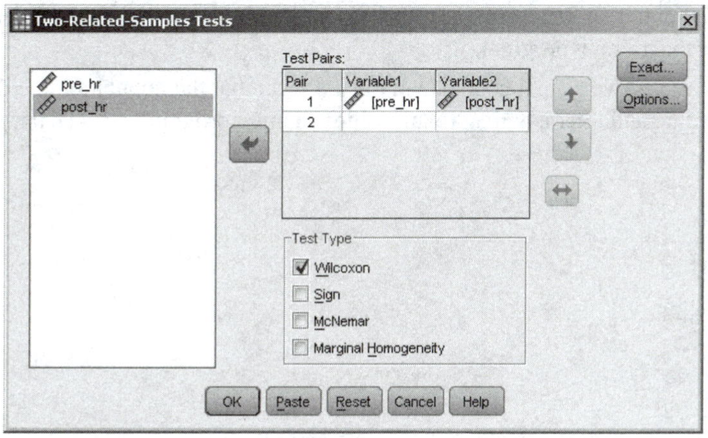

Figure 37.2 Completed *Two-Related-Samples Tests* dialog box.

4. Although not essential, you may click on the variable in the *Variable1* location and then click on the double-headed arrow to switch the variables located in the *Variable1* and *Variable2* locations. By switching locations in our example, the post_hr scores are subtracted from the pre_hr scores rather than vice versa. We chose not to make this switch.

5. Click *Options,* and you will see the *Two-Related-Samples: Options* dialog box in Figure 37.3.

6. Click *Descriptive* and click *Continue*.

7. Ensure that *Wilcoxon* is checked in the *Test Type* area.

8. Click *OK,* and you will see the partial results of the analysis in Figure 37.4.

Important Output and What It Means

- The mean and standard deviation of the pre_hr scores are 47.14 and 9.592, respectively. The mean and standard deviation of the post_hr scores are 50.04 and 10.858, respectively.

- The pre_hr scores are subtracted from the post_hr scores. Then these difference scores are rank ordered from smallest to largest regardless of sign. As shown on the *Output*, there are 14 difference scores with negative values, and their mean rank is 15.07. Also, there are 21 difference scores with positive values, and their mean rank is 19.95. Accordingly, the participants tended to self-report more empathy after the training program.

- Based on the results, we cannot conclude at the .05 level that the population medians on the empathy scale differ before and after a human relationships training program, $z = -1.705$, $p = .088$.

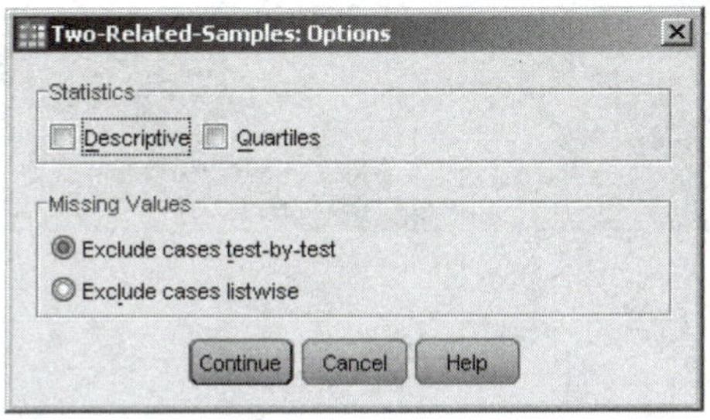

Figure 37.3 *Two-Related-Samples: Options* dialog box.

Wilcoxon Signed Ranks Test

Ranks

		N	Mean Rank	Sum of Ranks
post_hr - pre_hr	Negative Ranks	14[a]	15.07	211.00
	Positive Ranks	21[b]	19.95	419.00
	Ties	0[c]		
	Total	35		

a. post_hr < pre_hr

b. post_hr > pre_hr

c. post_hr = pre_hr

Test Statistics[b]

	post_hr - pre_hr
Z	-1.705[a]
Asymp. Sig. (2-tailed)	.088

a. Based on negative ranks.

b. Wilcoxon Signed Ranks Test

Figure 37.4 Partial results of the Wilcoxon test.

Index

Q

Qualitative variables
   in bivariate linear regression, 100
   descriptive statistics for, 58–61
   in discriminant analysis, 108–113
   See also Categorical variables
Quantitative variables
   in bivariate linear regression, 100–103
   descriptive statistics for, 62–65
   in discriminant analysis, 108–113
   in independent-samples t tests, 72–75
   in one-way ANOVA, 76–79
   in one-way repeated-measures ANOVA, 80–83
   Pearson product-moment correlation, 92–95

R

R^2, 98
Rank Cases command, 30, 32, 33f
Recoding, 30–32
Regressions
   bivariate linear, 100–103
   multiple linear, 100–103
Related samples, Wilcoxon test for two, 132–135
Reliability analysis, 118–121
Repeated-measures ANOVA, 80–83
Results pane, 51f, 52
Rotation, factor analysis, 114, 116, 117f
Rows, defined, 14

S

Sample eta squares, 78
Samples
   Mann-Whitney U test for two independent, 128–131
   Wilcoxon test for two related, 132–135
SAS data, importing/exporting, 24
Saving
   data files, 8, 9f
   output in *Viewer*, 56
Scale Statistics table, 120
Scales, defined, 62
Scatterplots
   bivariate, 94, 95f, 102, 103f
   multiple linear regression, 102, 103f
   partial correlation, 98, 99f
Scores
   sorting cases based on, 38, 39f
   transformations on, 30–33
   See also Analyses; Correlations; Regressions; *specific tests*
Scree plots, 114, 116, 117f
Search tab, 6, 7f

Select Cases command, 34, 35f
Selecting multiple items, 20, 21f
Showing results in *Contents* pane, 54
Significance (p-) values, 66, 70, 94, 98
Sort Cases command, 38, 39f
Spearman-Brown correlation, 120, 121f
Split File command, 34, 36, 37f
Split-half reliability coefficient, 118, 120, 121f
SPSS
   exiting, 22
   opening, 2–3
Standard deviations, 64, 65f
   See also Analyses; Correlations; Regressions; *specific tests*
Standard method
   binomial test, 122
   one-sample chi-square test, 126–127
Standardized mean differences, 66, 70, 74
Start up dialog box, 2, 3f
Statistics, descriptive. *See* Descriptive statistics
String type in one-sample t tests, 12
Structure Matrix
   in discriminant analysis, 108, 111f, 113f
   in factor analysis, 116
Summary Item Statistics table, 120

T

t tests
   independent-samples, 72–75
   one-sample, 66–67
   paired-samples, 68–71
Tables, 50–53
Test values in one-sample t tests, 66–67
Test variables
   in binomial test, 122–125
   in independent-samples t tests, 72–75
   in Mann-Whitney U test, 128–131
   in one-sample chi-square tests, 126–127
   in one-sample t tests, 66–67
Tests. *See* Chi-square tests; Nonparametric tests; t tests
Tests of Within-Subjects Effects table, 82, 83f
Toolbars, 4, 5f
Total Variance Explained table, 116, 115f
Transform menu option, defined, 4
Transforming data, 30–33
Two independent samples, Mann-Whitney U test for, 128–131
Two related samples, Wilcoxon test for, 132–135

Two-way ANOVA, 84, 86, 87f
Type property, 10, 11f, 12

U

Undoing actions, 18
Unequal Length, 120, 121f
Univariate ANOVA, 84, 86, 87f
Utilities menu option, defined, 4

V

Values property, 10, 11f, 12, 13f
Variable View tab, 2, 3f, 10, 11f
Variables
   control, in partial correlations, 100–103
   cutting/copying/pasting, 20
   defining properties of, 10–13
   deleting, 18, 19f, 20
   exporting, 26, 27f
   finding, 28, 29f
   finding values for, 28, 29f
   focal, 98, 99f
   inserting, 16, 17f
   mergingfiles with same/different, 40, 41f
   predictor, in discriminant analysis, 108–113
   selecting multiple, 20, 21f
   transformations into new, 30–33
   See also Analyses; Categorical variables; Classification variables; Correlations; Dependent variables; Factors; Grouping variables; Qualitative variables; Quantitative variables; Regressions; Test variables; *specific tests*
Variance, analysis of. *See* ANOVA
View menu option, defined, 4
Viewer
   using, 54–57
   viewing graphs in, 44, 45f
   viewing tables in, 51f, 52, 53f

W

Weighted cases method
   binomial test, 122–125
   one-sample chi-square test, 126
Width property, 10, 11f, 13f
Wilcoxon test, 132–135
Wilks' lambda
   in discriminant analysis, 108, 111
   in one-way repeated-measures ANOVA, 82, 83f
Window menu option, defined, 4
Within-subjects factors, 80–83

X

X^2 tests
   discriminant analysis and, 108
   one-sample, 126–127